John W. Harvey

Day book owned by John W. Harvey

Dairy for 1872

John W. Harvey

Day book owned by John W. Harvey
Dairy for 1872

ISBN/EAN: 9783337763145

Printed in Europe, USA, Canada, Australia, Japan

Cover: Foto ©ninafisch / pixelio.de

More available books at **www.hansebooks.com**

BANCROFT'S

FOR

1872,

CONTAINING

Useful Memoranda,

AND

TABLES FOR REFERENCE.

Published Annually.

SAN FRANCISCO:
A. L. BANCROFT & COMPANY,
BOOKSELLERS & STATIONERS,
721 MARKET STREET.
MDCCCLXXII.

CONTENTS.

	PAGE
Counting-House Calendar	3
Festivals and Fasts of the Church	4
Hebrew Calendar	5
Locations of Public Offices, Buildings, and Churches in San Francisco	6
San Francisco Fire Alarm Stations	14
Hack Fare in San Francisco	15
Distances from San Francisco	16
California State Stamp Tax	17
Note to Tides at San Francisco	17
United States Stamp Duties	18
Temperature of Various Localities	23
Important Epochs and Eras	23
Weights and Measures	24
Specific Gravity of Substances	25
The Metric System	26
Value of Foreign Coins	27
Rates of Postage	29
The Solar System	30
Time Table	31
Chronological Cycles	31
Eclipses	32
List of Sundays	32
Almanac	33

Entered according to Act of Congress, A. D. 1871,
BY A. L. BANCROFT & COMPANY,
In the office of the Librarian of Congress, at Washington.

Calendar,
1872.

	S	M	T	W	T	F	S
JAN.		1	2	3	4	5	6
	7	8	9	10	11	12	13
	14	15	16	17	18	19	20
	21	22	23	24	25	26	27
	28	29	30	31			
FEB.					1	2	3
	4	5	6	7	8	9	10
	11	12	13	14	15	16	17
	18	19	20	21	22	23	24
	25	26	27	28	29		
MAR.						1	2
	3	4	5	6	7	8	9
	10	11	12	13	14	15	16
	17	18	19	20	21	22	23
	24	25	26	27	28	29	30
	31						
APR.		1	2	3	4	5	6
	7	8	9	10	11	12	13
	14	15	16	17	18	19	20
	21	22	23	24	25	26	27
	28	29	30				
MAY				1	2	3	4
	5	6	7	8	9	10	11
	12	13	14	15	16	17	18
	19	20	21	22	23	24	25
	26	27	28	29	30	31	
JUNE							1
	2	3	4	5	6	7	8
	9	10	11	12	13	14	15
	16	17	18	19	20	21	22
	23	24	25	26	27	28	29
	30						

	S	M	T	W	T	F	S
JULY		1	2	3	4	5	6
	7	8	9	10	11	12	13
	14	15	16	17	18	19	20
	21	22	23	24	25	26	27
	28	29	30	31			
AUG.					1	2	3
	4	5	6	7	8	9	10
	11	12	13	14	15	16	17
	18	19	20	21	22	23	24
	25	26	27	28	29	30	31
SEP.	1	2	3	4	5	6	7
	8	9	10	11	12	13	14
	15	16	17	18	19	20	21
	22	23	24	25	26	27	28
	29	30					
OCT.			1	2	3	4	5
	6	7	8	9	10	11	12
	13	14	15	16	17	18	19
	20	21	22	23	24	25	26
	27	28	29	30	31		
NOV.						1	2
	3	4	5	6	7	8	9
	10	11	12	13	14	15	16
	17	18	19	20	21	22	23
	24	25	26	27	28	29	30
DEC.	1	2	3	4	5	6	7
	8	9	10	11	12	13	14
	15	16	17	18	19	20	21
	22	23	24	25	26	27	28
	29	30	31				

THE LENGTH OF DAYS.

At San Francisco the longest day has $14\frac{3}{4}$ hours; at Boston, $15\frac{1}{4}$; at Berlin and London, $16\frac{1}{2}$; at Stockholm and Upsal, $16\frac{1}{2}$; at Hamburg, Dantzic, and Stettin, 17, and the shortest 7. At St. Petersburg and Tobolsk the longest day has 19, and the shortest 5 hours. At Bornea, in Finland, the longest day has $21\frac{1}{2}$, and the shortest $2\frac{1}{2}$ hours. At Wanderbus, in Norway, the day lasts from the 21st of May to the 22d of July, without interruption; and at Spitzbergen, the longest day is $3\frac{1}{2}$ months.

FESTIVALS AND FASTS OF THE CHURCH.

Dates *italicized* apply only to 1872.

EPIPHANY is twelve days after Christmas, January 6th.

SHROVE SUNDAY, the first Sunday before Shrove Tuesday. — *February 11th.*

SHROVE TUESDAY is the first Tuesday after the first change of the moon in February. — *February 13th.*

ASH WEDNESDAY, the day after Shrove Tuesday. — *February 14th.*

The Fast of LENT is from Ash Wednesday to the feast of Easter, forty days.

The FIRST SUNDAY IN LENT is *February 18th.*

ST. PATRICK. — March 17th.

MIDLENT is the fourth Sunday from Shrove Tuesday. — *March 10th.*

CARLE SUNDAY, the fifth Sunday from Shrove Tuesday. — *March 17th.*

PALM SUNDAY, the 6th Sunday from Shrove Tuesday. — *March 24th.*

PASSION WEEK, the week after Palm Sunday. — *March 24th to March 31st.*

GOOD FRIDAY, the Friday in Passion Week. — *March 29th.*

EASTER DAY, the festival appointed in commemoration of Christ's Resurrection, is the seventh Sunday after Shrove Tuesday, or the first after the full moon, which happens on or after the 21st of March. — *March 31st.*

LOW SUNDAY is the first after Easter. — *April 7th.*

ROGATION SUNDAY is the fifth after Easter. — *May 5th.*

ASCENSION DAY, or HOLY THURSDAY, is the Thursday in Rogation Week, the fortieth day from Easter. — *May 9th.*

PENTECOST, or WHITSUNTIDE, is the forty-ninth day, or seventh Sunday after Easter. — *May 19th.*

TRINITY SUNDAY is the next after Pentecost. — *May 26th.*

ST. JOHN BAPTIST'S DAY. — June 24th.

ST. PETER. — June 29th.

ST. MICHAEL. — September 29th.

ALL SAINTS' DAY. — November 1st.

ADVENT SUNDAY, the nearest Sunday to the feast of St. Andrew. — *December 1st.*

ST. ANDREW. — November 30th.

ST. THOMAS. — December 21st.

CHRISTMAS. — December 25th.

ST. STEPHEN. — December 26th.

ST. JOHN, EVANGELIST. — December 27th.

HEBREW CALENDAR.
5632-5633.

[Prepared by Rev. J. Frankel.]

COMMENCEMENT { 5632, SEPTEMBER 16–17, 1871.
OF THE YEAR { 5633, OCTOBER 3–4, 1872.

| NEW MOONS. | FASTS AND FEASTS. | DATES. |

5632.   **1872.**

Shebat.................................Tues., Jan. 11.
Adar the First..................Fri. & Sat., Feb. 10–11.
Adar the First, 14...Purim Katan..........Fri., Feb. 23.
Adar the Second ....Sun. & Mon., March 10–11.
Adar the Second, 11. Fast of Esther........Th., March 21.
Adar the Second, 14–15. Purim. Sun. & Mon., March 24–25.
Neson................................Tu., April 9.
Neson, 15–22..Pesach..........Sun. to Sun., April 23–30.
Iyar..............................We. & Th., May 8–9.
Iyar, 18.......Lag Baomer..............Sun., May 26.
Sivan...................................Fri., June 7.
Sivan, 6–7....Shebuoth.........We. & Th., June 12–13.
Tammooz....................Sat. & Sun., July 6–7.
Tammooz, 17. Fast......................Tu., July 23.
Ab......................................Mon., Aug. 5.
Ab, 9.......Tishabeab — Fast.............Tu., Aug. 13.
Ab, 15.......Half Festival..............Mon., Aug. 19.
Ellool..........................Tu. & We., Sept. 3–4.

5633.

Tishree, 1–2..New Year............Th. & Fri., Oct. 3–4.
Tishree, 4....Fast of Gedaliah..............Sun., Oct. 6.
Tishree, 10...Yom - Kippur — Fast........Sat., Oct. 12.
Tishree, 15–16. Succoth—Tabernacles, Th. & Fri. Oct. 17–18.
Tishree, 21...Hoshaanah Rabbah..........Wed., Oct. 23.
Tishree, 22...Shemeenee Atzaroth..........Th., Oct. 24.
Tishree, 23...Simchath Torah.............Fri., Oct. 25.
Heshvon........................Fri. & Sat., Nov. 1–2.
Kislev..................................Sun., Dec. 1.
Kislev, 25....Hanucha, (first day),.........We., Dec. 25.
Tebeth,........................Mon. & Tu., Dec. 30–31.

LOCATIONS
OF
Public Offices and Buildings
IN
SAN FRANCISCO.

ACADEMY OF NATURAL SCIENCES, 622 Clay street.
ALMADEN QUICKSILVER CO., Office, 205 Battery street.
ARMY HEADQUARTERS, 417 Kearney, 509 Kearney, 204 Sutter
    S. W. cor. Market and Third sts.
ASSAY OFFICES:
    California Assay Office, 512 California st.
    Louis Falkenau, State Assayer, 421 Montgomery street.
    Henry G. Hanks, 649 Clay street.
    Hentsch & Berton, cor. Clay and Leidesdorff streets.
    Leopold Kuh, 611 Commercial street.
    Morris & White, 30 Fremont street.
    J. S. Phillips, 423 Washington street.
    F. Reichling & Co., 334 Montgomery street.
    Riehn, Hemme & Co., 404 Montgomery street.
    S. F. Assaying and Refining Works, 416 Montgomery st.
    W. L. Strong & Co., 10 Stevenson street.
    B. B. Thayer, 1 New Montgomery street.
ASYLUMS:
    Protestant Orphan, near Market street R. R.
    Roman Catholic Orphan, Market st., bet. Second and
        Third.
    Magdalen, San Bruno Road.
BANCROFT'S BOOK & STATIONERY MERCANTILE AND MANU-
    FACTURING ESTABLISHMENT, 721 Market street.
BANKS AND BANKERS:
    Bank of British Columbia, cor. California and Sansome
        streets.
    Bank of British North America, N. E. cor. California
        and Sansome sts.
    Bank of California, cor. California and Sansome sts.
    Belloc Freres, 524 Montgomery street.
    A. Borel & Co., cor. Montgomery and Jackson sts.
    California Trust Co., 421 California street.
    B. Davidson & Co., N. W. cor. Montgomery and Com-
        mercial streets.
    Donohoe, Kelly & Co., S.E. cor. Montgomery and Sac-
        ramento streets.

LOCATIONS OF PUBLIC OFFICES, ETC.

BANKS, (continued.)
    First National Bank, (Gold,) cor. Montgomery and Sacramento streets.
    Hentsch & Berton, cor. Clay and Leidesdorff streets.
    London and San Francisco Bank, 423 California st.
    Pacific Bank, N. W. cor. Sansome and Pine sts.
    Sather & Co., N.E. c. Montgomery and Commercial sts.
    J. Seligman & Co., 412 California street.
    Shepherd & Finnie, N. E. cor. California and Sansome.
    John Sime & Co., N.W. cor. Montgomery and Clay sts.
    Tallant & Co., 321 Battery street.
    Wells, Fargo & Co., N.W. c. Montgomery and California streets.

BIBLE DEPOSITORY, 757 Market street.

BOARD OF BROKERS, San Francisco Stock and Exchange, 411 California street.

BOARD OF EDUCATION, 22 City Hall, 2nd floor, op. the Plaza.

BOARD OF SUPERVISORS, Room 3 City Hall, op. the Plaza.

CALIFORNIA STEAM NAVIGATION CO., N. E. cor. Front and Jackson streets.

CHAMBER OF COMMERCE, New Merchants' Exchange, cor. California and Leidesdorff sts.

CHINA AND JAPAN STEAMERS, cor. First and Bryant sts.

CHURCHES :
    Baptist, First, north side Washington street, near Stockton.
    Baptist, Second, west side Russ st., bet. Howard and Folsom.
    Baptist, Third, (colored), east side Powell st., bet. Bush and Sutter.
    Baptist, Tabernacle, Post street, near Larkin.
    Baptist, Union Square, Post street, near Powell.
    Baptist, Fifth, Twenty-second st., near Howard.
    Chinese Mission House, N. E. cor. Sacramento and Stockton streets.
    Congregationalist, First, cor. Mason and Post streets.
    Congregationalist, Second, Taylor street, near Geary.
    Congregationalist, Third, Fifteenth street, near Mission.
    Congregationalist, Fourth, S. side Green, near Stockton street.
    Disciples, Church of Christ, 318 Post street.
    Episcopal, Grace, S.E. cor. California and Stockton sts.
    Episcopal, Trinity, N. E. cor. Post and Powell sts.
    Episcopal, St. John's, cor. Fifteenth and Valencia sts.
    Episcopal, Advent, Howard st., bet. Second and Third.
    Episcopal, St. James', Post street, near Mason.
    Episcopal, St. Luke's, Pacific st., near Polk.

CHURCHES, (*continued.*)

Hebrew, Emanu El, Sutter, b. Stockton and Powell sts.
Hebrew, Sherith Israel, east side Stockton street, bet. Broadway and Vallejo street.
Hebrew, Ohabai Shalome, Mason, bet. Geary and Post streets.
Hebrew, Beth Israel, Sutter street, near Stockton.
Lutheran, First, German, Mission street, bet. Second and Third.
Lutheran, St. Paul's, German, Mission st., bet. Fifth and Sixth.
Lutheran, St. Mark's, German, south side of Geary street, bet. Stockton and Powell.
Mariner's Church, cor. Sacramento and Drumm sts.
Methodist Episcopal, Powell Street, west side Powell street, bet. Washington and Jackson.
Methodist, Howard Street, Howard street, bet. Second and Third.
Methodist, Central, Mission st., bet. Sixth and Seventh.
Methodist, Mission Street, Mission st., bet. Eighteenth and Nineteenth.
Methodist, Seaman's Bethel, Mission street, bet. First and Second sts.
Methodist, Minna St., Minna st., bet. Fourth and Fifth.
Methodist, Kentucky St., on the Potrero, n. L. Bridge.
Methodist, Bernal Wesleyan, Prospect Avenue, Bernal Heights.
Methodist, South San Francisco, on Fifteenth avenue, S. S. F.
Methodist, German, Folsom st., bet. Fourth and Fifth.
Methodist, German, north side Broadway, bet. Stockton and Powell sts.
Methodist, African (colored), west side Powell, bet. Jackson and Pacific streets.
Methodist, Zion Wesleyan, (colored), Stockton st., near Sacramento.
Presbyterian, First, Stockton street, near Clay.
Presbyterian, Calvary, cor. Geary and Powell sts.
Presbyterian, Howard, S. side Mission st., near Third.
Presbyterian, Larkin Street, c. Larkin and Pacific sts.
Presbyterian, Central, Tyler st., near Taylor.
Presbyterian, Emanuel, corner Folsom and Sherman streets.
Presbyterian, Westminster, Fell street, b. Octavia and Laguna.

LOCATIONS OF PUBLIC OFFICES, ETC.

CHURCHES, (*continued*.)
    Presbyterian, United, Mason st., near Geary.
    Reformed Protestant, Excelsior Hall, 711 Mission st.
    Roman Catholic, St. Mary's Cathedral, N. E. cor. California and Dupont sts.
    Roman Catholic, St. Francis, Vallejo street, b. Dupont and Stockton sts.
    Roman Catholic, St. Patrick's, south side Market, bet. Second and Third streets.
    Roman Catholic, St. Boniface, (German,) north side Sutter, bet. Montgomery and Kearney streets.
    Roman Catholic, St. Ignatius, Market, bet. Fourth and Fifth streets.
    Roman Catholic, Notre Dame, (French), Bush, between Dupont and Stockton streets.
    Roman Catholic, Mission Dolores, S.W. cor. Sixteenth and Dolores sts.
    Roman Catholic, St. Joseph's, Tenth street, bet. Folsom and Howard sts.
    Roman Catholic, St. Rose's, Brannan st., near Fourth.
    Roman Catholic, St. Bridget's, S.W. cor. Van Ness Avenue and Broadway.
    St. Peter's, Columbia street, near Twenty-fourth.
    Spiritualists, Mechanics' Institute Hall, 29 Post st.
    Swedenborgian, New Jerusalem, O'Farrell street, bet. Mason and Taylor.
    Unitarian, First, Geary street, near Stockton.
CITY HALL, Kearney street, opposite the Plaza.
COAST SURVEY, Custom House, 3d floor, N. W. cor. Battery and Washington sts.
COMMISSIONER OF IMMIGRATION, 314 Washington street.
COURTS: Federal, U. S. Court Building, N. E. cor. Washington and Battery sts.
    District, County, and Probate, City Hall, op. the Plaza.
    Justices of the Peace, N. E. cor. Jackson and Montgomery sts., 2d floor.
CUSTOM HOUSE, N.W. cor. Battery and Washington streets.
DASHAWAY HALL, Post street, near Dupont.
EXPRESSES:
    Alameda and Contra-Costa, (Bamber & Co.) S. W. cor. Jackson and Davis streets.
    Half Moon Bay and Pescadero, and San Jose, Kennedy, Long & Co., 679 Market street.
    S. F. Package, General Office, 315 Montgomery st.
    San Rafael, W. L. Barnard, S. E. cor. Washington and Sansom sts.

BANCROFT'S DIARY.—1872.

EXPRESSES, (*continued*.)
    Wells, Fargo & Co., N. W. cor. California and Montgomery sts.

GAS COMPANY:
    San Francisco, Office, S. E. cor. First and Natoma sts.

HARBOR COMMISSIONERS, 414 Montgomery street.

HOSPITALS AND BENEVOLENT SOCIETIES:
    Alms House, near Lake Honda.
    British, 730 Montgomery street.
    County, S.W. cor. Francisco and Stockton streets.
    French Mutual Benevolent Society, 808 Montgomery st.
    German, 732 Washington street.
    Italian, 430 Jackson street.
    Marine, Rincon Point, cor. Mission and Fifteenth sts.
    San Francisco Female, 917 Clay street, cor. Prospect pl.
    S. F. Lying-in Hospital and Foundling Asylum, 269 Jessie street.
    St. Mary's Sisters of Mercy, cor. Bryant and First sts.

INDIAN AGENT, 224 Kearney street.

INDUSTRIAL SCHOOL, Office, City Hall, No. 9, third floor.

INTERNAL REVENUE:
    Assessor, 419 California ; Collector, 415 California ; Guagers, 321 Front ; Supervisor, S. E. cor. California and Sansome streets.

LADIES' PROTECTION AND RELIEF SOCIETY, Franklin Avenue, between Post and Geary streets.

LAND OFFICE, 506 Jackson street.

LIBRARIES:
    Mercantile, N. side Bush street, near Montgomery.
    Odd Fellows, 327 Montgomery, near California street.
    Mechanics' Institute, 27 Post st.
    San Francisco Law Library, 16 Exchange Building, N. E. cor Montgomery and Washington sts.

MARSHAL, U. S., 13 and 14 U. S. Court Building, N. E. cor. Washington and Battery streets.

MASONIC HALL, cor. Montgomery and Post streets.

MECHANICS' INSTITUTE, 27 Post street.

MERCHANTS' EXCHANGE, south side California street, near Montgomery.

MEXICAN STEAMSHIP LINE, Office, 217 Sansome street.

MINT, U. S. Branch, north side Commercial street, near Montgomery.

NEWSPAPER AND PERIODICAL OFFICES:
    Abend Post, (German, daily,) 521 Clay street.
    Advocate, (Methodist, weekly,) 711 Mission street.

LOCATIONS OF PUBLIC OFFICES, ETC.

NEWSPAPER AND PERIODICAL OFFICES, (*continued.*)
Alaska Herald, 611 Clay street.
Alta California, (daily,) 529 California street.
Bancroft's Guide for Travellers in the Pacific States and Territories, 721 Market street.
California Demokrat, (German, daily,) N. W. cor. Sacramento and Kearney sts.
California Farmer, (weekly,) 326 Clay street.
California Police Gazette, 525 Front street.
California Teacher, (monthly), cor. Pine and Montgomery streets.
Commercial Herald, 409 Washington street.
Commercial Record, 33 New Merchants' Exchange.
Courrier de San Francisco, (French,) 515 Jackson st.
El Tiempo, (Spanish, tri-weekly,) 411 Clay street.
Elevator, (colored, weekly,) 622 Battery street.
Evangel, (Baptist, weekly,) 608 Market street.
Evening Bulletin, (daily,) 622 Montgomery street.
Examiner, (daily,) 535 Washington street.
Figaro, (daily,) 532 Merchant street.
Golden City, (weekly,) 636 Sacramento street.
Golden Era, (weekly,) 543 Clay street.
Guide, 540 Clay street.
Hebrew, (weekly,) 420 Montgomery street.
Hebrew Observer, (weekly,) 502 Montgomery street.
Irish News, (weekly,) 432 Montgomery street.
L'Alouette, (French), 621 Sansom street.
La Voce del Popolo, (Italian,) 629 Washington street.
La Voz Nuevo Mondo, 728 Montgomery street.
L' Eco Della Patria, (Italian, semi-weekly,) 639 Washington street.
Le National, (French, weekly,) cor. Sansome and Jackson streets.
Masonic Mirror, (weekly,) 608 Market street.
Mining and Scientific Press, (weekly,) 414 Clay street.
Monitor, (Catholic, weekly.) 622 Clay street.
Morning Call, (daily,) 523 Montgomery street.
New Age. (I. O. O. F., weekly,) 325 Montgomery street.
Occident, (Presbyterian, weekly,) S. E. cor. Sacramento and Sansome streets.
Overland Monthly, 409 Washington street.
Pacific, (Congregationalist, weekly,) 409 Washington street.
Pacific Appeal, (colored, weekly,) 541 Merchant street.
Pacific Churchman, (Episcopal, weekly,) 536 Market st.

NEWSPAPER AND PERIODICAL OFFICES, (*continued.*)
    Pacific Medical and Surgical Journal, (monthly,) 26 Montgomery street.
    Pioneer, (weekly,) 420 Montgomery street.
    Real Estate Circular, (monthly,) 410 California street.
    San Francisco Chronicle, 504 Montgomery street.
    San Francisco News Letter, 623 Montgomery street.
    Spare Hour, (weekly,) 414 Clay street.
    Spectator, (Methodist, weekly,) 710 Washington street.
    Spirit of the Times, (weekly,) cor. Sansom and Jackson streets.
    Transcript of Records, (daily,) 317 California street.
ODD FELLOWS HALL, S.W. c. Montgomery and California sts.
OLYMPIC CLUB, Rooms, 35 Sutter street, near Montgomery.
OREGON STEAMSHIP LINE, Office, 217 Sansome street.
PACIFIC MAIL STEAMSHIP COMPANY, cor. First and Bryant streets.
PIONEER HALL, 808 Montgomery street, cor. Gold.
POLICE OFFICE, City Hall, opposite the Plaza.
POST OFFICE, Custom House, cor. Battery and Washington streets.
RAILROAD COMPANIES:
    California Pacific, corner Front and Vallejo streets; Office, 411 California street.
    Central Pacific, cor. Davis and Pacific; Office, 415 California street.
    S. F., San Jose and Gilroy, N. E. cor. Montgomery and Market streets.
RECORDER'S OFFICE, City Hall.
REGISTRAR IN BANKRUPTCY, 10 Court Block, 636 Clay street.
SAVINGS BANKS:
    Cosmopolitan Savings and Exchange Bank, 626 Montgomery st.
    Farmers' and Mechanics' Bank of Savings, 225 Sansom street.
    French Savings and Loan Mutual, 411 Bush st.
    Germania Savings and Loan, 513 California street.
    Hibernia Savings and Loan, N.E. cor. Montgomery and Market streets.
    Humboldt Savings and Loan, 16 Geary street.
    Improved Order of Red Men's Savings and Loan, 344 Bush street.
    Masonic Savings and Loan, 6 Post street.
    Odd Fellows' Savings and Loan, S.W. cor. Montgomery and California sts.

LOCATIONS OF PUBLIC OFFICES, ETC.

SAVINGS BANKS, (*continued.*)
    San Francisco Savings Union, 532 California street.
    Savings and Loan Society, 619 Clay street.
STEAMBOAT LANDINGS, Broadway Street Wharf.
STEAMER (Ocean) LANDINGS, cor. First and Bryant streets.
STREET RAILWAYS:
    Central, (Davis, Bush, Turk, and Sixth,) Office, 116 Taylor st., near Turk.
    City, (New Montgomery and Mission,) S. W. corner Mission and Fourteenth sts.
    Front Street, Mission, and Ocean, corner Bush and Polk streets.
    Market Street, N. E. cor. Market and Montgomery sts.
    North Beach and Mission, Fourth street, near Bryant, cor. Louisa.
    Omnibus, 721 Howard street, bet. Third and Fourth.
    Potrero and Bay View, cor. Fourth and Berry streets.
SURVEYOR GENERAL'S OFFICE, U. S., N. W. cor. Pine and Sansome streets.
TELEGRAPH OFFICES:
    Western Union, 522 California street.
    Atlantic and Pacific, 415 California street.
UNION HALL, Howard street, near Third.
UNITED STATES SUB-TREASURY, 428 Montgomery street.
WATER WORKS, Spring Valley, 516 California street.
YOUNG MEN'S CHRISTIAN ASSOCIATION, North side Sutter st., bet. Kearney and Dupont.

DIVISIONS OF TIME.

A SOLAR DAY is measured by the rotation of the earth upon its axis, and is of different lengths, owing to the ellipticity of the earth's orbit and other causes; but a mean solar day, recorded by the time-piece, is twenty-four hours long. An ASTRONOMICAL DAY commences at noon, and is counted from the first to the twenty-fourth hour. A CIVIL DAY commences at midnight, and is counted from the first to the twelfth hour, when it is recounted again from the first to the twelfth hour. A NAUTICAL DAY is counted as a civil day, but commences like an Astronomical Day, from noon.

A CALENDAR MONTH varies in length from 28 to 31 days. A MEAN LUNAR MONTH is 29 days, 12 hours, 44 minutes, 2 seconds, and 5.24 thirds.

A YEAR is divided into 365 days. A SOLAR YEAR, which is the time occupied by the Sun in passing from one Vernal Equinox to another, consists of 365.24244 solar days, or 365 days, 5 hours, 48 minutes, and 49.536 seconds. A JULIAN YEAR is 365 days. A GREGORIAN YEAR is 365.2425 days. Every fourth year is BISSEXTILE, or LEAP YEAR, and is 366 days.

SAN FRANCISCO
FIRE ALARM STATIONS.

FIRE ALARM BOXES are located at the corners of the following streets:

1. Stockton and Francisco
2. Mason and Lombard.
3. Stockton and Greenw'h.
4. Sansome and Greenw'h.
5. Battery and Union.
6. Montgomery and Green.
7. Kearney and Union.
8. Powell and Union.
9. Dupont and Vallejo.
12. California and Kearney.
13. Front and Broadway.
14. Stockton and Broadw'y.
15. Clay and East.
16. Pacific and Mason.
17. Pacific and Kearney.
18. Sansome and Jackson.
19. Washington and Davis.
21. City Hall.
23. Clay and Taylor.
24. Clay and Powell.
25. Washington & Dupont.
26. Clay and Battery.
27. Montgomery and Commercial.
28. Pine and Dupont.
29. Stockton and California.
31. California, n. Sansome.
32. California and Drumm.
34. Mission and Stewart.
35. Montgomery and Pine.
36. Folsom and Stewart.
37. Battery and Bush.
38. Market and Second.
39. Howard and Spear.
41. Sutter, near Jones.
42. Geary and Mason.
43. O'Farrell, near Dupont.
45. O'Farrell and Jones.
46. Kearney and Sutter.
47. Market and Powell
48. Market and Kearney.
49. Stockton and Sutter.
51. Folsom and Beale.
52. Mission and Fremont.
53. Townsend and Third.
54. Engine House, No. 4, Second st.
56. Bryant, west of First.
57. Brannan and Second.
58. Folsom and First.
59. P. M. S. S. Co.'s wharf, foot of Second.
61. Howard and Third.
62. Mission and Fourth.
63. Harrison and Fourth.
64. Howard and Fifth.
65. Mission and Sixth.
67. Harrison & Hawthorne.
68. Brannan and Fourth.
69. Bryant and Third.
71. Mission and Eleventh.
72. Mission and Thirteenth.
73. Howard and Eighth.
74. Engine No. 7, Sixteenth.
75. Market, opp. Seventh.
76. Market and Hayes.
78. Folsom and Ninth.
79. Folsom and Twelfth.
81. Franklin and Hayes.
82. Fulton and Gough.
83. Octavia and Oak.
84. Market and Valencia.
85. Laguna and Hayes.
91. Hyde and Turk.
92. Franklin and Turk.
93. Jones and Turk.
94. Polk and Ellis.
123. Hyde and Union.
124. Pioneer Woolen Mills.
125. Filbert and Jones.
126. Hyde and Washington.
127. Broadway and Polk.
128. Sacramento and Leavenworth.
129. Pacific & Leavenw'th.
132. Pine and Mason.
134. Bush and Hyde.
135. Bush and Polk.
136. Post and Van Ness av.
137. Post and Larkin.
138. California and Larkin.
139. O'Farrell and Hyde.
142. Valencia and Twent'th.
143. Mission and Twenty-second.
145. Folsom and Twenty-second.
146. Folsom and Sixteenth.
147. Howard and Twent'th.
148. Mission and Sixteenth.
149. Folsom and Eight'nth.
152. Brannan and Eighth.
153. Harrison and Seventh.
154. Bryant and Sixth.

FIRE ALARM STATIONS.

156. Fourth and Berry.	173. Ellis and Buchanan.
157. Folsom, east of Fourth.	174. Turk and Fillmore.
158. Folsom, east of Fifth.	213. Bush and Buchanan.
159. Engine House, No. 6, Sixth, near Folsom.	214. Bush and Steiner.
162. Pacific and Franklin.	231. Howard and Twenty-fourth.
163. Sacramento and Franklin.	234. Harrison and Twenty-fourth.
164. Clay and Polk.	
172. McAllister and Buchanan.	

HACK FARE IN SAN FRANCISCO.

ORDER No. 285, amending Section 4 of Order No. 43, regulating Hacks, Cabs, and other Vehicles in Public Streets.

RATES OF FARE.

For a Hack for one person, not exceeding one mile..	$1 50
For a Hack for two or more persons, not exceeding one mile..................................	2 50
For each additional mile, for each passenger.......	50
For a Cab for one person, not exceeding one mile...	1 00
For a Cab for two or more persons, not exceeding one mile..................................	1 50
For each passenger for each additional mile........	25
For a Cab for two persons, when engaged by the hour, to be computed for the time occupied in going and returning, including detention, for the first hour............................	1 50
For each subsequent hour so used.................	1 00
For a Hack for four or less persons, when engaged by the hour, to be computed for the time occupied in going and returning, including detention, for the first hour...................	3 00
For each subsequent hour so used.................	2 00

No extra charge to any passenger shall be made for the ordinary amount of baggage.

SEC. 5 OF ORDER 43.—"From the landing of any steamboat to any point east of the west line of Mason street, and north of the south line of Brannan street east of Third street, shall in all cases be estimated not to exceed one mile."

The penalty for the violation of any of the provisions of the above Order shall not be less than five dollars, nor more than ten dollars for each offence, exclusive of costs.

DISTANCES FROM SAN FRANCISCO

To various points in the vicinity of San Francisco Bay.

NAMES OF PLACES.	MS	CONVEYANCES.	TIME &C.
Fort Point	4	Street Railway	
Lone Mountain	3	" "	
Seal Rock	6	Cars & Omnibus	Two trips a day.
Dry Dock	6	Street Railways	
Ocean House	6	Private Carriage	
San Mateo	20	Railroad	
Crystal Springs	23	Railroad & Stage	} Stage from
Half Moon Bay	29	" "	} San Mateo.
Redwood City	30	Railroad	
Mountain View	38	"	
Santa Clara	47	"	
SAN JOSE	50	"	
Gilroy	80	"	
Almaden Mines	64	Railroad & Stage	Stage fm. San Jose.
Santa Cruz	78	" "	" " "
" "	80	Steamer	
OAKLAND	8	Ferry & R. R.	Eight trips a day.
Alameda	11	" "	Five trips a day.
San Leandro	15	" "	
Stockton	90	" "	Two trips a day.
Mission San Jose	30	" "	
Warm Springs	33	" "	
San Pablo	18	Steamer & Stage	Stage f. Pt. Isabel.
Sacramento	90	Steamer & R. R.	R. R. from Vallejo.
BENICIA	30	Steamer	} Leaves S. F. at
Sacramento	117	"	} 4 P. M., daily.
Stockton	117	"	
Martinez	33	"	Ferry fm. Benicia.
Pacheco	38	Steamer & Stage	} St'ge f. Martinez.
Diablo Coal Mines	44	" "	} Round trip d'ly.
Suisun City	50	Steamer	Tri-weekly.
Suisun	54	Steamer & R. R.	R. R. from Vallejo.
Vallejo & Mare Island	28	Steamer	Daily.
Napa City	50	Steamer & R. R.	R. R. from Vallejo.
Calistoga Springs	67	" "	" " "
Geyser Springs	118	St'r, R.R.& Stage	Stage fr. Calistoga
Sonoma	52	Steamer & Stage	Daily.
Petaluma	48	"	Daily.
Santa Rosa	64	Steamer & R. R.	R.R.fm. Petaluma.
Healdsburg	80	" "	" "
Geyser Springs	105	" "	" "
San Quentin	12	Steamer	Daily.
San Rafael	16	Steamer & R. R.	R. R. from S. Q.
Sauçilito	6	Ferry Boat	Passing Alcatraz.
Farallone Isls	21	Sail Boat	In the Ocean.

CALIFORNIA STATE STAMP TAX.

Rates of Stamp Tax on Bills of Exchange, Policies of Insurance, &c.

AMOUNTS TAXED.	Bills of Exchange.	Letters of Credit.	Policies of Insurance.
$20 to $50	$0 08	$0 08	$0 04
50 to 100	0 20	0 20	0 10
100 to 150	0 30	0 30	0 15
150 to 200	0 40	0 40	0 20
200 to 300	0 60	0 60	0 30
300 to 400	0 80	0 80	0 40
400 to 500	1 00	1 00	0 50
500 to 750	1 40	1 40	0 70
750 to 1,000	2 00	2 00	1 00
1,000 to 1,500	3 00	3 00	1 50
1,500 to 2,000	4 00	4 00	2 00
2,000 to 3,000	6 00	6 00	3 00
3,000 to 4,000	8 00	8 00	4 00
4,000 to 5,000	10 00	10 00	5 00
5,000 to 7,000	14 00	14 00	7 00
7,000 to 10,000	20 00	20 00	10 00
10,000 to 15,000	30 00	30 00	15 00
15,000 to 20,000	38 00	38 00	19 00
20,000 to 30,000	56 00	56 00	28 00
30,000 to 50,000	90 00	90 00	45 00
50,000 to 100,000	175 00	175 00	87 00
Above 100,000	200 00	200 00	100 00

Policies of Insurance, if for nine months and not less than six months, three fourths of the rates above charged; if for six months and not less than three months, one-half the rates above charged; if for three months or less, one-fourth the rates above charged.

Passengers' and Attorneys'.

First Class	$6 00
Second Class	4 00
Steerage	2 00
Attorneys'	10 00

TIDES AT SAN FRANCISCO.

NOTE. — The table of Tides for San Francisco are obtained from the latest data of the United States Coast Survey. These Tides are extremely irregular, both as regards interval and height. The two daily tides may occur either during the same morning, or during the same afternoon. In the tide columns of these pages the asterisk (*) denotes the second morning tide, and the obelisk (†) the first afternoon tide of the day when so occurring. Finally, the larger tide of the day is distinguished by the letter (*l*), and the smaller by (*s*).

A COMPLETE
Table of Stamp Duties.

AGREEMENT, or CONTRACT, not otherwise specified; any appraisement of value or damage, or for other purpose; for each agreement, or for each sheet of each agreement, or renewal of same... $0.05

ASSIGNMENT.— See conveyance.

BANK CHECK, DRAFT, or ORDER for the payment of any sum of money drawn upon any bank, banker, or trust company, or for any sum exceeding $10, drawn upon any other person, companies, or corporations, at sight or on demand.......... .02

BILL OF EXCHANGE, (*Inland,*) DRAFT, or ORDER, for the payment of money, not at sight or on demand, or any PROMISSORY NOTE (except bank notes issued for circulation, and checks made and intended to be forthwith presented, and which shall be presented to a bank or banker for payment,) or any memorandum, check, receipt, or other written or printed evidence of money to be paid on demand, or at a time designated, for every $100 or part thereof.......... .05

BILL OF EXCHANGE, (*Foreign,*) or LETTERS OF CREDIT, drawn in but payable out of the United States:
  If drawn singly or in duplicate, same as Inland bills of Exchange.
  If drawn in sets of three or more, every bill of each set, for every $100, or the equivalent thereof, in any foreign currency in which the bill is expressed.............................. .02

BILL OF LADING, or RECEIPT, (other than charter party,) for any goods &c., exported to a foreign port... .10

BILL OF SALE OF VESSEL, or any part thereof, consideration of value not over $500 .... .50
Every add'l $500, or part thereof, 50 cents more.

BOND OF INDEMNITY, every $1,000, or part thereof.. .50

BOND, for the execution of the duties of any office.. 1.00

UNITED STATES STAMP DUTIES.

BOND, other than required in legal proceedings, or used in connection with mortgage deeds, and not otherwise charged....................	.25
CERTIFICATE OF STOCK, in incorporated company....	.25
CERTIFICATE OF PROFITS, or any certificate or memorandum showing an interest in the property or accumulations of any incorporated company, if for $10 and not over $50....................	.10
Over $50 and not over $1,000............	.25
Every add'l $1,000, or part thereof, 25 cents more.	
CERTIFICATE OF DAMAGE, or otherwise, and all other certificates or documents issued by any port warden, marine surveyor, or person acting as such..	.25
CERTIFICATE OF DEPOSIT, $100 or less.............	.02
Over $100..................................	.05
(Certificates of measurement or weight of animals, wood, coal, or hay; certificate of the record of a deed or other instrument in writing, or of the acknowledgment or proof thereof, by attesting witnesses, require no stamp.)	
CERTIFICATE, of any description not specified above..	.05
CHARTER PARTY, (or renewal &c. of same,) contract or agreement for charter of vessel or steamer of registered tonnage, not over 150 tons.........	1.00
Over 150 and not over 300 tons.............	3.00
Over 300 and not over 600 tons.............	5.00
Over 600 tons.............................	10.00
CONTRACT, or renewal, Broker's note, or memorandum of sale of merchandise, exchange, real estate, or other property issued by brokers, or persons acting as such, each.................	.10
CONVEYANCE.—Deed or writing, whereby any lands, tenements, or other realty sold is granted, assigned, or transferred, for every $500, or part thereof......................................	.50
ENTRY OF GOODS, &c., at any custom house, for consumption or warehousing, of value not over $100	.25
Over $100 and not over $500	.50
Over 500...............................	1.00
WITHDRAWAL from bonded warehouse...........	.50
INSURANCE (*Life*).—Policy, (or assignment, &c. of same,) not over $1,000.....................	.25
Over $1,000 and not over $5000...........	.50
Over 5,000.............................	1.00

INSURANCE, (*Marine, Inland, and Fire*).—Each policy or renewal, (or assignment, &c. of same,) on which premium is $10 or less............ .10
 Over $10 and not over $50................. .25
 Over 50................................. .50

INSURANCE against accidental injury to persons, exempt.

LEASE, agreement, memorandum, or contract, for the hire, use, or rent of any land, tenement, or portion thereof, when rent or rental value is not over $300 per annum....................... .50
Every add'l $200, or part thereof, 50 cents more.

LEASE, ASSIGNMENT OF.—A stamp duty equal to that imposed on the original instrument, increased by a stamp duty on the consideration or value of the assignment equal to that imposed upon the conveyance of land for similar consideration of value. (See Conveyance.)

MANIFEST, for custom house entry or clearance of vessel's cargo for foreign port, (except British North America,) tonnage not over 300 tons..... 1.00
 Over 300 and not over 600 tons............. 3.00
 Over 600 tons............................ 5.00

MORTGAGE, Trust Deed, or Personal Bond, for the payment of money, over $100 and not over $500 .50
Every add'l $500, or part thereof, 50 cents more.
Upon each assignment or transfer of a mortgage, a stamp duty equal to that upon a mortgage for the amount remaining unpaid.
TRUST DEED conveying estate to uses, to be stamped as a conveyance.

OFFICIAL INSTRUMENTS, documents and papers issued by the officers of the United States government, or by the officers of any State, county or town, require no stamp.
Affidavits in suits or legal proceedings, exempt.

ORDER for the payment of money.—See Bank Check.

PASSAGE TICKET, to foreign port, costing $35 or less. .50
 Over $35 and not over $50................. 1.00
Every add'l $50, or part thereof, $1 more.

PROTEST of note, bill of exchange, acceptance, check or draft, or any marine protest, whether protested by a notary public or by any other officer who may be authorized by law to make such protest, .25

UNITED STATES STAMP DUTIES.

Power of Attorney, to sell or transfer any stock, bond, or scrip, or for the collection of any dividend, or interest thereon .... .25
    To vote by proxy for officers of any corporation or society, (except religious, charitable, literary societies, or public cemeteries,)................ .10
    To sell or rent real estate...................... 1.00
    To collect rents................................ .25
    To perform any act not herein mentioned........ .50

Probate of Will, or Letters of Administration, value of estate not over $2,000................ 1.00
    Every add'l $1,000, or part thereof, 50 cents more. (Probate of will, letters testamentary or of administration, or administrator's or guardian's bonds, when the value of the estate, real and personal, does not exceed $1,000, require no stamp.)

Promissory Note.— For a less sum than $100, exempt.

Receipt for any sum of money, or for the payment of any debt, exempt.

Warehouse Receipt, exempt.

Proprietary, Medicines, Perfumery, Cosmetics, Preparations, &c., each package retailed at not over 25 cents .... .01
    Over 25 cents and not over 50 cents .... .02
    Over 50 cents and not over 75 cents .... .03
    Over 75 cents and not over $1.............. .04
Every add'l 50 cents, or part thereof, 2 cents more.

Friction Matches, or lucifer matches, or other articles made in part of wood, and used for like purposes, each package of 100 matches or part thereof....................................... .01
Packages of more than 100 matches, for each 100 or part thereof............................. .01

Cigar Lights, made in part of wood, wax, glass, paper, or other materials, in packages containing twenty-five lights or less, each package........ .01
Every additional twenty-five lights or part thereof, 1 cent more.

Playing Cards, for and upon every pack, not exceeding fifty-two cards in number, irrespective of price or value............................ .05

CANNED MEATS, &c., for and upon every can, bottle or other single package, containing meats, fruits, vegetables, sauces, sirups, prepared mustard, jams or jellies, not exceeding 2 lbs. in weight... .01
Every additn'l pound or part thereof, 1 cent more.

The indiscriminate use of all kinds of stamps (except postage or proprietary) is permitted, care being taken to affix a stamp or stamps of the proper amount.

Documents made in any foreign country, to be used in the United States, shall pay the same duty as when made here.

Powers of Attorney, or other papers relating to applications for bounties, arrearages of pay, or pensions, require no stamp ; neither do indorsement of negotiable instrument, nor any warrant of attorney accompanying a bond or note when such bond or note shall be stamped ; and whenever any bond or note shall be secured by mortgage, but one stamp duty is required, provided the stamp duty placed thereon is the highest rate required for said instrument, or either of them.

The person using or affixing the stamp or stamps, shall write thereupon the initials of his name and the date upon which the same shall be attached or used, so that the same shall not be used again, under a penalty of $50 ; or they may be otherwise canceled as the Commissioner of Internal Revenue may prescribe.

Violations of these Stamp Duties will be punished as the law directs.

TEMPERATURE OF VARIOUS LOCALITIES.

PLACE.	LATITUDE	MEAN TEMPERATURE.		
		OF YEAR	OF WINT'R	OF SUM'R
Algiers	36° 48'	69.98°	61.52°	80.24°
Amsterdam	52.22	51.62	36.86	65.84
Berne	46.05	49.28	32.00	66.56
Bourdeaux	44.50	56.48	42.08	70.88
Brussels	50.50	51.80	36.68	66.20
Cairo	30.02	72.32	58.46	85.10
Cambridge, U.S.	42.25	50.86	33.98	70.70
Cincinnati	39.06	53.78	32.90	72.86
Copenhagen	55.41	45.68	30.74	62.60
Dublin	53.21	49.10	39.20	59.54
Edinburgh	55.57	47.84	38.66	58.28
Geneva	46.12	49.28	34.70	64.94
Havana	23.10	78.08	71.24	83.30
London	51.30	50.36	39.56	63.14
Marsailles	43.17	59.00	45.50	72.50
Moscow	55.45	40.10	10.78	67.10
Nagasaki	32.45	60.80	39.38	82.94
Natchez	31.28	64.76	48.56	79.16
New York	40.40	53.78	29.84	79.16
Paris	48.50	51.08	38.66	64.58
Pekin	39.54	54.86	26.42	82.58
Philadelphia	39.56	53.42	32.18	73.94
Quebec	46.47	41.74	14.18	68.00
Rome	41.53	60.44	45.86	75.20
Sacramento	38.32	59.90	48.46	70.77
San Francisco	37.47	55.85	50.59	58.97
Stockholm	59.20	42.26	25.52	61.88
St. Petersburg	59.56	38.84	17.06	62.06
Vera Cruz	19.11	77.72	71.96	81.50
Vienna	48.12	50.54	32.72	69.26
Warsaw	52.14	48.56	28.76	69.08

IMPORTANT EPOCHS AND ERAS,

WITH THE PERIODS OF THEIR COMMENCEMENT.

———:o:———

Grecian Year of the World............September 1, B. C. 5598.
Julian Period............................January 1, B. C. 4713.
Jewish Mundane Era...............Vernal Equinox, B. C. 3761.
Destruction of Troy........................June, B. C. 1184.
Building of Solomon's Temple.................May, B. C. 1015.
Era of Olympiads......New Moon, Summer Solstice, B. C. 776.
Roman Era..............................April 24, B. C. 753.
Era of Nabonasser......................February 26, B. C. 747.
Metonic Cycle.............................July 15, B. C. 432.
Julian Year..............................January 1, B. C. 45.
Augustan Era..........................February 14, B. C. 27.
Indiction of Constantinople..............September 1, B. C. 3.
Christian Era..................January 1, A. D. 1; A. M. 4004.
Destruction of Jerusalem...............September 21, A. D. 69.
Era of Diocletian......................September 17, A. D. 284.
Era of Hegira.............................July 16, A. D. 622.
Persian Era................................June 16, A. D. 632.
Conquest of England ....October 14, A. D. 1066.
Declaration American Independence ....July 4, A. D. 1776.

WEIGHTS AND MEASURES.

WEIGHT OF UNITED STATES COINS.

	Grains.	Ounces.		Grains.	Ounces.
Double Eagle	= 516	= 1.075	3-Dollar piece	= 77.4	= .16125
Eagle........	= 258	= 0.5375	Quarter Eagle	= 64.5	= .144375
Half-Eagle...	= 129	= 0.26875	Dollar piece..	= 25.8	= .05375

The ounce of Gold is valued at $18.6046.
The ounce of Silver is valued at $1.25.

TROY WEIGHT.

Pound.		Ounces.		Pennyweights.		Grains.		Pounds Avoir.
1	=	12	=	240	=	5,760	=	.822861
..		1	=	20	=	480	=	.068571
..		..		1	=	24	=	.0034285

AVOIRDUPOIS WEIGHT.

Ton.		Cwt.		Pounds.		Ounces.		Drams.
1	=	20	=	2,240	=	35,840	=	573,440
..		1	=	112	=	1,792	=	28,672
..		..		1	=	16	=	256
..		..		..		1	=	16

APOTHECARIES' WEIGHT.

Pound.		Ounces.		Drams.		Scruples.		Grains.
1	=	12	=	96	=	288	=	5,760
..		1	=	8	=	24	=	480
..		..		1	=	3	=	60
..		..		..		1	=	20

LIQUID CAPACITY.

Gallon.		Quarts.		Pints.		Gills.		Cubic Inches.
1	=	4	=	8	=	32	=	231.
..		1	=	2	=	8	=	57.75
..		..		1	=	4	=	28.875
..		..		..		1	=	7.2175

A cylinder 7 inches in diameter and 6 inches high, holds a gallon.
A cubic foot contains 6.232 gallons.

DRY CAPACITY.

1 Bushel = 4 Pecks = 8 Gallons = 32 Quarts = 2150.42 Cubic Inches.

A cylinder 18.5 inches in diameter and 8 inches deep, holds a bushel.

WEIGHTS AND MEASURES.

MEASURES OF LENGTH.

Mile.	Furlongs.	Chains.	Rods.	Yards.	Feet.	Inches.
1 =	8 =	80 =	320 =	1,760 =	5,280 =	63,360
	1 =	10 =	40 =	220 =	660 =	7,920
		1 =	4 =	22 =	66 =	792
			1 =	5.5 =	16.5 =	198
				1 =	3 =	36
					1 =	12

1 Statute Mile = 5,280 feet = .86275 Nautical Miles.
1 Nautical Mile = 6,120 feet = 1.15908 Statute Miles.
60 Nautical Miles = 69.545 Statute Miles.
1 Cable Length = 120 Fathoms = 240 Yards = 720 Feet.

MEASURES OF SURFACE.

Sq. Mile.	Acres.	Sq. Chains.	Sq. Rods.	Sq. Yards.	Sq. Feet.
1 =	640 =	6,400 =	102,400 =	3,097,600 =	27,878,400
	1 =	10 =	160 =	4,840 =	43,560
		1 =	16 =	484 =	4,356
			1 =	30.25 =	272.25
				1 =	9

A lot 220 by 198 feet = 1 Acre.
A 50-vara lot, San Francisco measurement, is 137½ feet square. A 100-vara lot is 275 feet square. The San Francisco Vara is 2 feet 9 inches. The true Vara is 2.781 feet. A San Francisco 100-vara lot = 1.7367 Acres.

DRAWING PAPER.

Cap..............13 × 16 in.	Columbier........23 × 33¾ in.
Demy...........15½ × 19¼ "	Atlas ....26 × 33 "
Medium ....18 × 22 "	Theorem ....28 × 34 "
Royal...........19 × 24 "	Double Elephant..26 × 40 "
Super-royal......19 × 27 "	Antiquarian .....31 × 53 "
Imperial.........21¼ × 29 "	Emperor........40 × 60 "
Elephant ....22¼ × 27¾ "	Uncle Sam ......48 × 120 "

SPECIFIC GRAVITY OF SUBSTANCES.

Barometer, 30 in.; Fahren. Thermometer, 60 deg.

Platinum, wire.........21.04	Aluminium 2.56
Gold, British standard...17.49	Glass, flint.........2.8 to 3.6
Mercury 13.57	Limestone ....2.4 to 3.0
Lead..................11.35	Slate..............2.1 to 2.9
Silver.................10.51	Marble, Parian.........2.84
Copper............8.8 to 8.9	Granite..........2.65 to 2.75
Brass.............7.8 to 8.7	Chalk...........2.2 to 2.7
Steel..................7.83	Ivory 1.83
Iron, wrought...........7.79	Mahogany..............1.06
Iron, cast..............7.21	India Rubber...........0.93
Tin....................7.30	Proof Spirit............0.92
Zinc..............6.2 to 7.2	Alcohol, pure..........0.79
Antimony...............6.7	Cork..................0.24

THE METRIC SYSTEM.

MEASURES OF LENGTH.

Metric Denominations and Values.			Equivalents in Denominations in use.
Myriameter	=	10,000 meters	= 6.2137 miles.
Kilometer	=	1,000 meters	= 0.62137 m., or 3,280 ft., 10 in.
Hectometer	=	100 meters	= 328 feet and 1 inch.
Dekameter	=	10 meters	= 393.7 inches.
Meter	=	1 meter	= 39.37 inches.
Decimeter	=	.1 of a meter	= 3.937 inches.
Centimeter	=	.01 of a meter	= 0.3937 inch.
Millimeter	=	.001 of a meter	= 0.0394 inch.

MEASURES OF SURFACE.

Metric Denominations and Values.			Equivalents in Denominations in use.
Hectare	=	10,000 square meters	= 2.471 acres.
Are	=	100 square meters	= 119.6 square yards.
Centare	=	1 square meter	= 1550 square inches.

MEASURES OF CAPACITY.

Metric Denominations and Values.				Equivalents in Denominations in use.	
NAMES.	NO. OF LITERS.	CUBIC MEASURE.	DRY MEASURE.	WINE MEASURE.	
Kiloliter or stere	= 1,000	= 1 cubic meter	= 1.308 cubic yds.	= 264.17 galls.	
Hectoliter	= 100	= .1 cubic meter	= 2 bush., 3.35 pks.	= 26.417 galls.	
Dekaliter	= 10	= 10 c. decimet's	= 9.08 quarts	= 2.6417 galls.	
Liter	= 1	= 1 cu. decimeter	= 0.908 quart	= 1.0567 qurts.	
Deciliter	= .1	= .1 c. decimeter	= 6.1022 cubic ins.	= 0.845 gill.	
Centiliter	= .01	= 10 c. centimet's	= 0.6102 cubic in.	0.338 fl'id oz.	
Milliliter	= .001	= 1 c. centimeter	= 0.061 cubic inch	= 0.27 fluid dr.	

WEIGHTS.

Metric Denominations and Values.			Equivalents in Denominations in use.	
Names.	No. grams.	Weight of what quantity of water at maxim'm density.	Avoirdupois Weight.	
Millier or tonneau	= 1,000,000	= 1 cubic meter	= 2204.6 pounds.	
Quintal	= 100,000	= 1 hectoliter	= 220.46 pounds.	
Myriagram	= 10,000	= 10 liters	= 22.046 pounds.	
Kilogram or kilo	= 1,000	= 1 liter	= 2.2046 pounds.	
Hectogram	= 100	= 1 deciliter	= 3.5274 ounces.	
Dekagram	= 10	= 10 c. centimet's	= 0.3527 ounce.	
Gram	= 1	= 1 c. centimeter	= 15.432 grains.	
Decigram	= .1	= .1 c. centimeter	= 1.5432 grains.	
Centigram	= .01	= 10 c. millimet's	= 0.1543 grain.	
Milligram	= .001	= 1 c. millimeter	= 0.0154 grain.	

VALUE OF
FOREIGN GOLD AND SILVER COINS.

			D.	C.	M.
AUSTRIA	Gold,	Quadruple Ducat	9	12	0
"	"	Ducat	2	27	5
"	"	Sovereign (for Lombardy)	6	75	0
"	Silver,	Rix Dollar	0	97	0
"	"	Florin	0	48	5
"	"	Twenty Kreutzers	0	16	0
"	"	Lira (for Lombardy)	0	16	0
BADEN	Gold,	Five Gulden	2	04	0
"	Silver,	Crown	1	07	0
"	"	Gulden, or Florin	0	39	5
BAVARIA	Gold,	Ducat	2	27	0
"	Silver,	Crown	1	06	5
"	"	Florin	0	39	5
"	"	Six Kreutzers	0	03	0
BELGIUM	Gold,	Twenty-franc piece	3	83	2
"	"	Twenty-five-Franc piece	4	72	0
"	Silver,	Five Francs	0	93	0
"	"	Two-and-a-half Francs	0	46	5
"	"	Two Francs	0	37	0
"	"	Franc	0	18	5
BOLIVIA	Gold,	Doubloon	15	58	0
"	Silver,	Dollar	1	00	6
"	"	Half Dollar (debased, 1830)	0	37	5
"	"	Quar. Dollar (debased, 1830)	0	18	7
BRAZIL	Gold,	Piece of 6400 Reis	8	72	0
"	Silver,	Twelve hundred Reis	0	99	2
"	"	Eight hundred Reis	0	66	0
"	"	Four Hundred Reis	0	33	0
BREMEN	Silver,	Thirty-six Grote	0	35	6
BRITAIN	Gold,	Sovereign	4	84	5
"	Silver,	Half Crown	0	54	0
"	"	Shilling	0	21	7
"	"	Sixpence	0	10	8
"	"	Fourpence	0	07	1
BRUNSWICK	Gold,	Ten Thaler	7	80	0
"	Silver,	Thaler	0	68	0
CENT'L AMERICA,	Gold,	Doubloon	14	96	0
"	"	Escudo	1	67	0
"	Silver,	Dollar (about)	0	67	0
COSTA RICA	Gold,	Half Doubloon (1850)	7	62	0
"	Silver,	New Real	0	05	8
CHILI	Gold,	Doubloon (before 1835)	15	57	0
"	"	Doubloon (1835, and since)	15	66	0
"	Silver,	Dollar	1	01	0
"	"	Quarter Dollar	0	22	4
"	"	Eighth Dollar, or Real	0	11	2
DENMARK	Gold,	Double Fred. or Ten Thaler	7	88	0
"	Silver,	Rigshank Daler	0	52	3
"	"	Specie Daler	1	04	7
"	"	Thirty-two Skillings	0	17	0
ECUADOR	Gold,	Half Doubloon	7	60	0
"	Silver,	Quarter Dollar	0	18	7
EGYPT	Gold,	Hundred Piastres	4	97	0
"	Silver,	Twenty Piastres	0	96	0
FRANCE	Gold,	Twenty Francs	3	85	0
"	Silver,	Five Francs	0	93	2
"	"	Franc	0	18	5
FRANKFORT	Silver,	Florin	0	39	5
GREECE	Gold,	Twenty Drachms	3	45	0
"	Silver,	Drachm	0	16	0
GUIANA, BRITISH,	Silver,	Guilder	0	26	2
HANOVER	Gold,	Ten Thaler	7	89	0
"	Silver,	Thaler (fine silver)	0	99	2
"	"	Thaler (750 fine)	0	68	0
HAYTI	Silver,	Dollar, or 100 Centimes	0	25	7

VALUE OF FOREIGN COINS.

			D.	C.	M.
HESSE CASSEL...	Silver,	Thaler	0	67	5
"		One-sixth Thaler	0	11	0
HESSE DARMSTADT,	"	Florin, or Gulden	0	39	,
HINDOSTAN	Gold,	Mohur (E. I. Co.)	7	10	0
"	Silver,	Rupee	0	44	5
MECKLENBURG...	Gold,	Ten Thaler	7	89	0
MEXICO	Gold,	Doubloon (average)	15	53	0
"	Silver,	Dollar (average)	1	00	7
NAPLES	Silver,	Scudo	0	94	0
NETHERLANDS...	Gold,	Ducat	2	26	5
"		Ten Guilders	4	00	7
"	Silver,	Three Guilders	1	20	0
"		Guilder	0	40	0
"		Twenty-five Cents	0	09	5
"		Two-and-a-half Guilders	0	98	2
NEW GRANADA...	Gold,	Doubloon, 21 carat stand.,	15	61	0
"		" includ'g the silver,	15	66	0
"		" nine-tenths stand.,	15	31	0
"		" includ'g the silver,	15	36	0
"	Silver,	Dollar, usual weight	1	02	0
"		Dollar, or Ten Reals, 1851	0	93	0
NORWAY	Silver,	Rigsdaler	1	05	0
PERSIA	Gold,	Tomann	2	23	0
"	Silver,	Sahib Koran	0	21	5
PERU	Gold,	Doubloon, Lima, to 1833	15	55	0
"		Doubloon, Cuzco, to 1833	15	62	0
"		Doubloon, Cuzco, 1837	15	53	0
"	Silver,	Dollar, Lima mint	1	00	6
"		Dollar, Cuzco	1	00	8
"		Half Dollar, Cuzco, debased	0	36	0
"		Half Dollar, Arequipa, "	0	36	0
"		Half Dollar, Pasco	0	49	5
POLAND	Silver,	Zloty	0	11	2
PORTUGAL	Gold,	Half Joe (full weight)	8	65	0
"		Crown	5	81	0
"	Silver,	Cruzado	0	55	2
"		Crown of 1000 Reis	1	12	0
"		Half Crown	0	56	0
PRUSSIA	Gold,	Double Frederick	8	00	0
"	Silver,	Thaler, average	0	68	0
"		One-sixth Thaler, average	0	11	0
"		Double Thaler, or 3½ Gulden	1	39	0
ROME	Gold,	Ten Scudi	10	37	0
"	Silver,	Scudo	1	00	5
"		Teston (3-10 Scudo)	0	30	0
RUSSIA	Gold,	Five Roubles	3	96	7
"	Silver,	Rouble	0	75	0
"		Ten Zloty	1	13	5
"		Thirty Copecks	0	22	0
SARDINIA	Gold,	Twenty Lire	3	84	5
"	Silver,	Five Lire	0	93	2
SAXONY	Gold,	Ten Thaler	7	94	0
"		Ducat	2	26	0
"	Silver,	Species Thaler	0	96	0
"		Thaler (XIV. F.M.)	0	68	0
SIAM	Silver,	Tical	0	58	5
SPAIN	Gold,	Pistole (Quarter Doubloon)	3	90	5
"	Silver,	Pistareen (4 Reals Vellon..)	0	19	5
SWEDEN	Silver,	Species Daler	1	04	2
"		Half Daler	0	52	0
TURKEY	Gold,	Hundred Piastres	4	37	4
"		Twenty Piastres (new)	0	82	0
"	Silver,	Twenty Piastres (new)	0	82	0
TUSCANY	Gold,	Sequin	2	30	0
"	Silver,	Leopoldone	1	05	0
"		Florin	0	26	2
WURTEMBERG...	Silver,	Gulden, 1824	0	38	5
"		Gulden, 1838, and since	0	39	5
" .		Double Thaler, or 3½ Gulden	1	39	0

RATES OF POSTAGE.

LETTERS TO ANY PART OF THE UNITED STATES, 3 cents for each 1-2 ounce or part thereof.

DROP LETTERS, 2 cents per each half ounce.

ADVERTISED LETTERS, 1 cent, in addition to the regular rates.

VALUABLE LETTERS may be registered on application at the office of mailing, and the payment of a registration fee of 20 cents.

TRANSIENT NEWSPAPERS, Periodicals, Pamphlets, Blanks, Proof Sheets, Book Manuscripts, and all mailable printed matter, (except circulars and books,) 2 cents for each and every 4 ounces. Double these rates are charged for Books.

UNSEALED CIRCULARS, (to one address,) not exceeding 3 in number, 2 cents, and in the same proportion for a greater number.

SEEDS, CUTTINGS, ROOTS, &c., 2 cents for each 4 ounces or less quantity. Weight not to exceed 4 lbs.

ALL PACKAGES of Mail Matter not charged with letter postage must be so arranged that the same can be *conveniently* examined by Postmasters; if not, letter postage will be charged.

NO PACKAGE will be forwarded by mail which weighs over 4 pounds.

ALL MAILABLE MATTER, for delivery within the United States, except newspapers sent to regular subscribers, must be PREPAID by stamps, except duly certified letters of soldiers and sailors.

WEEKLY NEWSPAPERS, (one copy only,) sent to actual Subscribers within the County where printed and published, *free*. This does not include papers published in the City and circulated in the City.

LETTERS TO BRITISH COLUMBIA, MEXICO, JAPAN, CHINA, MANILA, AND SANDWICH ISLANDS, 10 cents for each 1-2 ounce. Prepayment required. Postage on newspapers, 2 cents.

LETTERS TO PANAMA AND ASPINWALL, 10 cents for each 1-2 ounce; papers, 2 cents each.

LETTERS TO AUSTRALIA, NEW ZEALAND, AND TASMANIA, 10 cents for each 1-2 ounce.

LETTERS TO THE DOMINION OF CANADA, 6 cents for each 1-2 ounce if prepaid, and 10 cents if unpaid.

LETTERS TO GREAT BRITAIN OR IRELAND, 6 cents for each 1-2 ounce. Prepayment optional; but, if unpaid, subject to a fine.

LETTERS TO OTHER FOREIGN COUNTRIES vary in rate according to the route by which they are sent, and the proper information can be obtained of any Postmaster in the United States.

THE SOLAR SYSTEM.

The Sun, the centre of the Solar System, has a diameter of 885,680 miles, and its bulk is 1,400,000 times greater than that of the Earth, and 700 times greater than that of all the bodies revolving around it.

THE PLANETS.

Name.	Diameter in Miles.	Volume.	Distance from Sun.	Period of Revolution.
Mercury,	2,950	1–19	36,000,000	3 mos.
Venus,	7,800	9–10	67,000,000	7½ mos.
Earth,	7,912	1	92,000,000	1 yr.
Mars,	4,500	1–6	140,000,000	2 yrs.
Asteroids,	(approximate)		250,000,000	4½ yrs.
Jupiter,	89,000	1,400	480,000,000	12 yrs.
Saturn,	79,000	1,000	876,000,000	29 yrs.
Uranus,	35,000	86	1,762,000,000	84 yrs.
Neptune,	31,000	60	2,760,000,000	164 yrs.

The Moon's diameter is 2,160 miles, and her volume one forty-ninth of that of the Earth. She revolves in her orbit once in 29½ days, at a distance of 240,000 miles from the Earth.

The Asteroids exceed one hundred in number. Leverrier estimates that their aggregate mass does not exceed one-third of that of the Earth.

VELOCITY OF THE EARTH'S MOTION.—The Earth moves forward in its orbit, 1,640,000 miles per day, 68,000 miles per hour, 1,100 miles per minute, and nearly 19 miles every second.

APPARENT TIME is reckoned by the revolutions of the Sun from the meridian to the meridian again. These intervals being unequal, of course the apparent solar days are unequal to each other.

MEAN TIME is time reckoned by the *average* length of all the solar days throughout the year. This is the period which constitutes the civil day of 24 hours.

TIME TABLE.

Time of day at various places on the globe when it is 12 o'clock (noon) at San Francisco.

A. M.	H M S	P. M.	H M S
Astoria, Oregon..	11 54 12	Halifax, N. S......	3 55 36
Calcutta, India....	1 35 56	Havana, Cuba.....	2 41 00
Canton, China....	3 43 00	Jerusalem, Pal....	10 31 24
Honolulu, S. I....	9 39 8	Lima, Peru.......	3 1 36
Melbourne, Aust..	5 48 00	London, Eng......	8 9 31
Pekin, China......	3 56 00	Los Angelos, Cal...	12 16 80
Sydney, Australia .	6 14 00	Louisville, Ky.....	2 27 4
Singapore, E. I....	3 8 00	Mexico, Mex......	1 33 44
Shanghai, China...	4 12 40	Mecca, Ara.......	10 50 00
Tobolsk, Siberia...	12 43 00	Montreal, Canada..	3 15 44
Yedo, Japan......	5 30 00	New Orleans, La...	2 9 40
Yreka, Cal........	11 59 30	New York City....	3 14 00
		Nevada, Cal.......	12 5 15
P. M.		Oregon City, Ore ..	12 0 40
Acapulco, Mex ..,	1 26 28	Panama, Isthmus.	2 52 40
Archangel, Russia.	10 50 00	Paris, France.....	8 19 24
Aspinwall, Isthm's.	2 50 40	Philadelphia, Pa...	3 9 22
Berlin, Prus......	9 3 35	Placerville, Cal....	12 6 18
Boston, Mass.....	3 25 48	Portland, Me......	3 29 8
Cape Good Hope..	9 32 50	Rio Janeiro, Brazil.	5 17 8
Charleston, S. C...	2 50 40	Rome, Italy.......	9 0 3
Chicago, Ill.......	2 19 44	Sacramento, Cal...	12 3 58
Cincinnati, O......	2 32 16	Santa Fe, N. Mex. .	12 55 44
Constantinople....	10 9 44	Salt Lake City	12 41 40
Detroit, Mich.....	2 38 12	St. Louis, Mo.....	2 9 4
Eastport, Maine...	3 42 00	St. Petersburg....	10 11 20
Fort Yuma, Cal...	12 31 18	Stockholm, Swd'n.	9 22 20
Frankfort, Ger....	8 43 24	Toronto, Canada...	2 52 00
Galveston, Tex....	1 50 32	Vienna, Austria...	9 15 35
Geneva, Switz.....	8 34 42	Washington, D.C..	3 2 00
Gibraltar, Spain...	7 48 44		

At the Isle of France, Indian Ocean, it is midnight when it is noon at San Francisco.

CHRONOLOGICAL CYCLES, 1872.

Dominical Letters.......	G.F.	Lunar Cycle or Golden No.	11
Epact...................	20	Roman Indiction........	15
Solar Cycle	5	Julian Period...........	6,585

ECLIPSES IN THE YEAR 1872.

In the year 1872 there will be four Eclipses; two of the Sun, and two of the Moon.

I.— A PARTIAL ECLIPSE OF THE MOON, May 22d, invisible to California. Visible, more or less, to Europe, Asia, Africa, South America, and eastern edge of North America.

II.— AN ANNULAR ECLIPSE OF THE SUN, June 6th, invisible to North America. Visible to Asia.

III.— A PARTIAL ECLIPSE OF THE MOON, November 14th, visible at San Francisco as follows:

Moon enters Penumbra	6	52 after.
Moon enters Shadow	8	52 "
Middle of Eclipse	9	10 "
Moon leaves Shadow	9	27 "
Moon leaves Penumbra	11	27 "

IV.— A TOTAL ECLIPSE OF THE SUN, November 30th, invisible to North America. Visible to southern part of South America and South Pacific Ocean.

Morning and Evening Stars.

VENUS will be *Morning Star* until July 16th; and *Evening Star* the rest of the year.

JUPITER will be *Morning Star* until January 15th; then *Evening Star* till August 2d, and *Morning Star* again the rest of the year.

List of Sundays in 1872.

JANUARY	7	14	21	28	
FEBRUARY	4	11	18	25	
MARCH	3	10	17	24	31
APRIL	7	14	21	28	
MAY	5	12	19	26	
JUNE	2	9	16	23	30
JULY	7	14	21	28	
AUGUST	4	11	18	25	
SEPTEMBER	1	8	15	22	29
OCTOBER	6	13	20	27	
NOVEMBER	3	10	17	24	
DECEMBER	1	8	15	22	29

ALMANAC FOR 1872.

January.
MOON'S PHASES.
Last Quarter, 3d. 1h. 49m. A.
New Moon, 10d. 6h. 48m. M.
First Quarter, 17d. 3h. 52m. M.
Full Moon, 25d. 9h. 4m. M.

February.
MOON'S PHASES.
Last Quarter, 2d. 2h. 0m. M.
New Moon, 8d. 5h. 42m. A.
First Quarter, 15d. 10h. 14m. A.
Full Moon, 24d. 2h. 46m. M.

D of M	D of W	Sun Rises h m	Sun Sets h m	Days' Length h m	Moon R & S h m	D of M	D of W	Sun Rises h m	Sun Sets h m	Days' Length h m	Moon R & S h m
1	Mo	7 16	4 51	9 35	10 29	1	Th	7 4	5 24	10 20	morn
2	Tu	7 16	4 52	9 36	11 30	2	Fr	7 3	5 25	10 22	0 36
3	We	7 16	4 54	9 38	morn	3	Sa	7 2	5 27	10 25	1 45
4	Th	7 16	4 55	9 39	0 33	4	S	7 1	5 28	10 27	2 55
5	Fr	7 16	4 56	9 40	1 39	5	Mo	7 0	5 29	10 29	4 4
6	Sa	7 16	4 57	9 41	2 49	6	Tu	6 59	5 30	10 31	5 11
7	S	7 16	4 58	9 42	4 1	7	We	6 58	5 31	10 33	6 12
8	Mo	7 16	4 59	9 43	5 14	8	Th	6 57	5 33	10 36	sets
9	Tu	7 15	5 0	9 45	6 27	9	Fr	6 56	5 34	10 38	6 30
10	We	7 15	5 1	9 46	sets	10	Sa	6 55	5 35	10 40	7 41
11	Th	7 15	5 2	9 47	6 30	11	S	6 54	5 36	10 42	8 50
12	Fr	7 15	5 3	9 48	7 44	12	Mo	6 53	5 37	10 44	9 57
13	Sa	7 15	5 4	9 49	8 56	13	Tu	6 52	5 38	10 46	11 1
14	S	7 14	5 5	9 51	10 6	14	We	6 51	5 39	10 48	morn
15	Mo	7 14	5 6	9 52	11 10	15	Th	6 50	5 40	10 50	0 2
16	Tu	7 14	5 7	9 53	morn	16	Fr	6 49	5 41	10 52	1 3
17	We	7 14	5 8	9 54	0 12	17	Sa	6 48	5 42	10 54	2 2
18	Th	7 13	5 9	9 56	1 13	18	S	6 46	5 43	10 57	2 59
19	Fr	7 13	5 10	9 57	2 13	19	Mo	6 45	5 44	10 59	3 52
20	Sa	7 12	5 11	9 59	3 12	20	Tu	6 44	5 45	11 1	4 42
21	S	7 12	5 12	10 0	4 10	21	We	6 43	5 46	11 3	5 26
22	Mo	7 11	5 13	10 2	5 6	22	Th	6 41	5 47	11 6	6 5
23	Tu	7 11	5 14	10 3	5 58	23	Fr	6 40	5 48	11 8	rises
24	We	7 10	5 16	10 6	6 46	24	Sa	6 38	5 49	11 11	6 15
25	Th	7 10	5 17	10 7	rises	25	S	6 37	5 50	11 13	7 17
26	Fr	7 9	5 18	10 9	6 20	26	Mo	6 36	5 51	11 15	8 19
27	Sa	7 8	5 19	10 11	7 22	27	Tu	6 34	5 52	11 18	9 23
28	S	7 7	5 20	10 13	8 24	28	We	6 33	5 53	11 20	10 28
29	Mo	7 7	5 21	10 14	9 25	29	Th	6 31	5 54	11 23	11 36
30	Tu	7 6	5 22	10 16	10 26						
31	We	7 5	5 23	10 18	11 30						

HIGH TIDES :: JANUARY.

D	Morn'g	Even'g	D	Morn'g	Even'g
1	4 33s	3 25l	17	6 18s	6 22l
2	5 15s	4 30l	18	6 50l	7 40s
3	6 0s	5 40s	19	7 27l	8 53s
4	6 54l	6 49s	20	8 2l	10 2s
5	7 28l	7 57s	21	8 35l	11 1s
6	8 7l	9 0s	22	9 6l	
7	8 43l	10 31s	23	0 0s	9 34l*
8	9 31l	11 38s	24	0 34s	10 01*
9	10 12l		25	1 7s	10 46l*
10	0 42s	10 42l*	26	1 34s	11 41l*
11	1 30s	11 38l*	27	2 15s	0 30l
12	2 27s	0 30l	28	2 44s	1 17l
13	3 11s	1 37l	29	3 7s	2 11l
14	3 56s	2 42l	30	3 35s	3 12l
15	4 41s	3 51l	31	4 26l	4 13s
16	5 34l	5 10l		*For	explan

HIGH TIDES :: FEBRUARY.

D	Morn'g	Even'g	D	Morn'g	Even'g
1	4 55l	5 29s	16	5 34l	7 34s
2	5 30l	6 47s	17	6 0l	8 35s
3	6 21l	8 7s	18	6 50l	9 50s
4	7 7l	9 28s	19	7 37l	10 37s
5	8 2l	10 44s	20	8 25l	11 23s
6	8 50l	11 45s	21	9 10l	11 58s
7	9 45l		22	9 55l	
8	0 35s	10 47l*	23	0 20s	10 38l*
9	1 20s	11 46l*	24	0 52s	11 39l*
10	1 59s	0 45l	25	1 29s	0 29l
11	2 31s	1 41l	26	1 53s	1 17l
12	3 1s	2 37l	27	2 31l	2 2s
13	3 35s	3 39l	28	2 44l	3 0s
14	4 13l	5 3s	29	3 10l	4 12s
15	4 52l	6 18s			

atory remarks, see Note on page 17

ALMANAC FOR 1872.

March.

MOON'S PHASES.

Last Quarter, 2d. 11h. 18m. M.
New Moon, 9d. 4h. 43m. M.
First Quarter, 15d. 6h. 15m. A.
Full Moon, 24d. 5h. 33m. A.
Last Quarter, 31d. 6h. 21m. A.

D of M	D of W	Sun Rises h m	Sun Sets h m	Days' Length h m	Moon R & S h m
1	Fr	6 30	5 55	11 25	morn
2	Sa	6 29	5 56	11 27	0 47
3	S	6 27	5 57	11 30	1 54
4	Mo	6 26	5 58	11 32	2 59
5	Tu	6 24	5 59	11 35	3 59
6	We	6 23	6 0	11 37	4 52
7	Th	6 21	6 1	11 40	5 37
8	Fr	6 20	6 2	11 42	6 14
9	Sa	6 18	6 3	11 45	sets
10	S	6 17	6 4	11 47	7 36
11	Mo	6 15	6 5	11 50	8 43
12	Tu	6 14	6 6	11 52	9 48
13	We	6 12	6 7	11 55	10 49
14	Th	6 11	6 7	11 56	11 50
15	Fr	6 9	6 8	11 59	morn
16	Sa	6 8	6 9	12 1	0 49
17	S	6 6	6 10	12 4	1 45
18	Mo	6 5	6 11	12 6	2 37
19	Tu	6 3	6 12	12 9	3 24
20	We	6 2	6 13	12 11	4 4
21	Th	6 0	6 14	12 14	4 40
22	Fr	5 58	6 15	12 17	5 11
23	Sa	5 56	6 16	12 20	5 42
24	S	5 55	6 17	12 22	rises
25	Mo	5 53	6 18	12 25	7 13
26	Tu	5 52	6 19	12 27	8 18
27	We	5 51	6 20	12 29	9 27
28	Th	5 49	6 21	12 32	10 37
29	Fr	5 48	6 21	12 33	11 45
30	Sa	5 46	6 22	12 36	morn
31	S	5 45	6 23	12 38	0 53

April.

MOON'S PHASES.

New Moon, 7d. 4h. 21m. A.
First Quarter, 15d. 2h. 1m. A.
Full Moon, 23d. 5h. 27m. M
Last Quarter, 30d. 0h. 11m. M.

D of M	D of W	Sun Rises h m	Sun Sets h m	Days' Length h m	Moon R & S h m
1	Mo	5 43	6 24	12 41	1 54
2	Tu	5 42	6 25	12 43	2 49
3	We	5 40	6 26	12 46	3 34
4	Th	5 39	6 27	12 48	4 13
5	Fr	5 37	6 28	12 51	4 47
6	Sa	5 36	6 29	12 53	5 17
7	S	5 34	6 30	12 56	sets
8	Mo	5 33	6 30	12 57	7 31
9	Tu	5 31	6 31	13 0	8 34
10	We	5 30	6 32	13 2	9 36
11	Th	5 29	6 33	13 4	10 38
12	Fr	5 27	6 34	13 7	11 36
13	Sa	5 26	6 35	13 9	morn
14	S	5 24	6 36	13 12	0 29
15	Mo	5 23	6 37	13 14	1 17
16	Tu	5 22	6 38	13 16	1 59
17	We	5 20	6 39	13 19	2 38
18	Th	5 19	6 40	13 21	3 13
19	Fr	5 17	6 41	13 24	3 42
20	Sa	5 16	6 42	13 26	4 10
21	S	5 15	6 43	13 28	4 36
22	Mo	5 14	6 44	13 30	5 4
23	Tu	5 12	6 44	13 32	rises
24	We	5 11	6 45	13 34	8 23
25	Th	5 10	6 46	13 36	9 35
26	Fr	5 9	6 47	13 38	10 45
27	Sa	5 8	6 48	13 40	11 51
28	S	5 6	6 49	13 43	morn
29	Mo	5 5	6 50	13 45	0 48
30	Tu	5 4	6 51	13 47	1 36

HIGH TIDES::MARCH.

D	Morn'g	Even'g	D	Morn'g	Even'g
1	3 40*l*	5 35s	17	5 7*l*	8 7s
2	4 35*l*	6 55s	18	6 4*l*	9 2s
3	5 29*l*	8 18s	19	7 4*l*	9 52s
4	6 24*l*	9 34s	20	8 4*l*	10 39s
5	7 34*l*	10 39s	21	8 56*l*	11 10s
6	8 41*l*	11 30s	22	9 47*l*	11 37s
7	9 42*l*		23	10 34*l*	11 58s
8	0 10s	10 56*l*	24	11 21*l*	
9	0 42s	11 52*l*	25	0 17*l*	0 5s
10	1 14s	0 50*l*	26	1 19*l*	0 58s
11	1 39s	1 43*l*	27	1 40*l*	1 52s
12	1 56*l*	2 46s	28	2 2*l*	2 53s
13	2 29*l*	3 46s	29	2 27*l*	4 5s
14	2 50*l*	4 50s	30	3 5*l*	5 30s
15	3 31*l*	5 56s	31	4 4*l*	6 58s
16	4 10*l*	7 13s			

HIGH TIDES::APRIL.

D	Morn'g	Even'g	D	Morn'g	Even'g
1	5 4*l*	8 15s	16	5 30*l*	8 18s
2	6 15*l*	9 27s	17	6 34*l*	9 7s
3	7 29*l*	10 20s	18	7 36*l*	9 50s
4	8 38*l*	11 10s	19	8 34*l*	10 24s
5	9 36*l*	11 42s	20	9 29*l*	10 53s
6	10 28*l*		21	10 19*l*	11 15s
7	0 8s	11 44*l*	22	11 8*l*	11 36s
8	0 33s	0 37*l*	23	11 49s	11 59*l*
9	0 49*l*	1 39s	24		1 7s
10	1 11*l*	2 37s	25	0 41*l*	2 7s
11	1 31*l*	3 31s	26	1 7*l*	3 7s
12	1 57*l*	4 23s	27	1 41*l*	4 20s
13	2 38*l*	5 32s	28	2 26*l*	5 30s
14	3 29*l*	6 29s	29	3 39*l*	6 55s
15	4 28*l*	7 26s	30	4 57*l*	8 2s

ALMANAC FOR 1872.

May.

MOON'S PHASES.
New Moon, 7d. 5h. 8m. M.
First Quarter, 15d. 7h. 55m. M.
Full Moon, 22d. 2h. 58m. A.
Last Quarter, 29d. 6h. 2m. M.

D of M	D of W	Sun Rises h m	Sun Sets h m	Days' Length h m	Moon R & S h m
1	We	5 8	6 52	13 49	2 16
2	Th	5 2	6 53	13 51	2 51
3	Fr	5 0	6 53	13 53	3 20
4	Sa	4 59	6 54	13 55	3 49
5	S	4 58	6 55	13 57	4 16
6	Mo	4 57	6 56	13 59	4 43
7	Tu	4 56	6 57	14 1	sets
8	We	4 55	6 58	14 3	8 26
9	Th	4 54	6 59	14 5	9 24
10	Fr	4 53	7 0	14 7	10 20
11	Sa	4 52	7 1	14 9	11 11
12	S	4 51	7 2	14 11	11 57
13	Mo	4 51	7 2	14 11	morn
14	Tu	4 50	7 3	14 13	0 36
15	We	4 49	7 4	14 15	1 11
16	Th	4 48	7 5	14 17	1 41
17	Fr	4 47	7 6	14 19	2 9
18	Sa	4 47	7 6	14 19	2 36
19	S	4 46	7 7	14 21	3 3
20	Mo	4 45	7 8	14 23	3 31
21	Tu	4 44	7 9	14 25	4 2
22	We	4 44	7 10	14 26	4 35
23	Th	4 43	7 10	14 27	rises
24	Fr	4 43	7 11	14 28	9 37
25	Sa	4 42	7 12	14 30	10 39
26	S	4 42	7 13	14 31	11 32
27	Mo	4 41	7 14	14 33	morn
28	Tu	4 41	7 14	14 33	0 16
29	We	4 40	7 15	14 35	0 53
30	Th	4 40	7 16	14 36	1 25
31	Fr	4 40	7 17	14 37	1 54

June.

MOON'S PHASES.
New Moon, 5d. 7h. 13m. A.
First Quarter, 13d. 11h. 9m. A.
Full Moon, 20d. 10h. 47m. A.
Last Quarter, 27d. 1h. 17m. A.

D of M	D of W	Sun Rises h m	Sun Sets h m	Days' Length h m	Moon R & S h m
1	Sa	4 39	7 17	14 38	2 20
2	S	4 39	7 18	14 39	2 45
3	Mo	4 39	7 18	14 39	3 12
4	Tu	4 38	7 19	14 41	3 43
5	We	4 38	7 19	14 41	4 17
6	Th	4 38	7 20	14 42	sets
7	Fr	4 37	7 20	14 43	9 7
8	Sa	4 37	7 21	14 44	9 54
9	S	4 37	7 21	14 44	10 36
10	Mo	4 37	7 21	14 44	11 12
11	Tu	4 37	7 22	14 45	11 42
12	We	4 37	7 22	14 45	morn
13	Th	4 37	7 23	14 46	0 11
14	Fr	4 37	7 23	14 46	0 38
15	Sa	4 37	7 23	14 46	1 4
16	S	4 37	7 24	14 47	1 29
17	Mo	4 38	7 24	14 47	1 57
18	Tu	4 38	7 25	14 47	2 28
19	We	4 38	7 25	14 47	3 6
20	Th	4 38	7 25	14 47	3 52
21	Fr	4 38	7 25	14 47	rises
22	Sa	4 39	7 25	14 47	9 22
23	S	4 39	7 26	14 47	10 11
24	Mo	4 39	7 26	14 47	10 53
25	Tu	4 39	7 26	14 47	11 26
26	We	4 40	7 26	14 46	11 56
27	Th	4 40	7 26	14 46	morn
28	Fr	4 41	7 26	14 45	0 24
29	Sa	4 41	7 26	14 45	0 51
30	S	4 41	7 26	14 45	1 18

HIGH TIDES :: MAY.

D	Morn'g	Even'g	D	Morn'g	Even'g
1	6 14l	9 2s	17	7 15l	8 39s
2	7 28l	9 50s	18	8 19l	9 15s
3	8 36l	10 26s	19	9 19l	9 47s
4	9 36l	10 54s	20	10 8s	10 18l
5	10 40s	11 9l	21	11 4s	10 38l
6	11 27s	11 48l	22	0 1s†	11 1l
7	0 16s†	11 48l	23	1 19s†	11 53l
8		1 14s	24		2 20s
9	0 9l	2 35s	25	0 26l	3 16s
10	0 34l	3 28s	26	1 16l	4 15s
11	1 3l	4 3s	27	2 17l	5 24s
12	1 48l	4 46s	28	3 36l	6 32s
13	2 50l	5 38s	29	4 58l	7 27s
14	3 57l	6 13l	30	6 13l	8 14s
15	5 6l	7 20s	31	7 24l	8 55s
16	6 10l	8 0s			

HIGH TIDES :: JUNE.

D	Morn'g	Even'g	D	Morn'g	Even'g
1	8 31l	9 30s	16	7 48l	8 16s
2	9 16s	10 5l	17	8 48s	8 58l
3	10 23s	10 28l	18	9 54s	9 28l
4	11 18s	10 46l	19	11 0s	10 0l
5	0 12s†	11 4l	20	0 2s†	10 36l
6	1 4s†	11 34l	21	1 21s†	11 27l
7		2 0s	22		2 15s
8	0 0l	3 0s	23	0 15l	3 7s
9	0 38l	3 36s	24	1 9l	3 58s
10	1 23l	4 11s	25	2 10l	4 56s
11	2 20l	4 54s	26	3 22l	5 53s
12	3 22l	5 36s	27	4 39l	6 43s
13	4 32l	6 22s	28	5 53l	7 24s
14	5 37l	7 1s	29	7 10l	7 58l
15	6 41l	7 37s	30	8 10l	8 34l

ALMANAC FOR 1872.

July.
MOON'S PHASES.
New Moon, 5d. 10h. 15m. M.
First Quarter, 13d. 11h. 38m. M.
Full Moon, 20d. 5h. 43m. M.
Last Quarter, 26d. 11h. 8m. A.

D of M	D of W	Sun Rises h m	Sun Sets h m	Days' Length h m	Moon R & S h m
1	Mo	4 42	7 26	14 44	1 48
2	Tu	4 42	7 25	14 43	2 20
3	We	4 43	7 25	14 42	2 56
4	Th	4 43	7 25	14 42	3 40
5	Fr	4 44	7 24	14 40	sets
6	Sa	4 44	7 24	14 40	8 34
7	S	4 45	7 24	14 39	9 12
8	Mo	4 45	7 23	14 38	9 45
9	Tu	4 46	7 23	14 37	10 13
10	We	4 47	7 23	14 36	10 40
11	Th	4 48	7 22	14 34	11 6
12	Fr	4 48	7 22	14 34	11 32
13	Sa	4 49	7 21	14 32	11 58
14	S	4 50	7 21	14 31	morn
15	Mo	4 51	7 20	14 29	0 27
16	Tu	4 52	7 20	14 28	1 0
17	We	4 52	7 19	14 27	1 40
18	Th	4 53	7 19	14 26	2 30
19	Fr	4 54	7 18	14 24	3 31
20	Sa	4 55	7 17	14 22	rises
21	S	4 56	7 16	14 20	8 45
22	Mo	4 56	7 16	14 20	9 24
23	Tu	4 57	7 15	14 18	9 56
24	We	4 58	7 14	14 16	10 26
25	Th	4 59	7 13	14 14	10 53
26	Fr	5 0	7 12	14 12	11 20
27	Sa	5 0	7 12	14 12	11 50
28	S	5 1	7 11	14 10	morn
29	Mo	5 2	7 10	14 8	0 20
30	Tu	5 3	7 9	14 6	0 57
31	We	5 4	7 8	14 4	1 37

August.
MOON'S PHASES.
New Moon, 4d. 1h. 35m. M.
First Quarter, 11d. 9h. 42m. A.
Full Moon, 18d. 0h. 43m. A.
Last Quarter, 25d. 0h. 25m. A.

D of M	D of W	Sun Rises h m	Sun Sets h m	Days' Length h m	Moon R & S h m
1	Th	5 4	7 14	3	2 24
2	Fr	5 5	7 6	14 1	3 15
3	Sa	5 6	7 5	13 59	4 11
4	S	5 7	7 4	13 57	sets
5	Mo	5 8	7 3	13 55	8 17
6	Tu	5 8	7 1	13 53	8 44
7	We	5 9	7 0	13 51	9 9
8	Th	5 10	6 59	13 49	9 34
9	Fr	5 11	6 58	13 47	10 0
10	Sa	5 12	6 57	13 45	10 27
11	S	5 13	6 56	13 43	10 57
12	Mo	5 14	6 54	13 40	11 33
13	Tu	5 15	6 53	13 38	morn
14	We	5 16	6 52	13 36	0 17
15	Th	5 17	6 51	13 34	1 12
16	Fr	5 17	6 49	13 32	2 17
17	Sa	5 18	6 48	13 30	3 31
18	S	5 19	6 47	13 28	rises
19	Mo	5 20	6 46	13 26	7 51
20	Tu	5 21	6 44	13 23	8 23
21	We	5 22	6 43	13 21	8 53
22	Th	5 23	6 41	13 18	9 21
23	Fr	5 24	6 40	13 16	9 49
24	Sa	5 25	6 39	13 14	10 20
25	S	5 26	6 37	13 11	10 54
26	Mo	5 26	6 36	13 10	11 34
27	Tu	5 27	6 34	13 7	morn
28	We	5 28	6 33	13 5	0 19
29	Th	5 29	6 32	13 3	1 9
30	Fr	5 30	6 30	13 0	2 4
31	Sa	5 30	6 29	12 59	3 2

HIGH TIDES::JULY.

D	Morn'g	Even'g	D	Morn'g	Even'g
1	9 24s	9 2l	17	10 17s	8 23l
2	10 28s	9 29l	18	11 27s	9 27l
3	11 20s	9 56l	19	0 22s†	10 24l
4	0 22s†	10 19l	20	1 9s†	11 21l
5	1 13s†	10 59l	21		1 52s
6	1 50s†	11 39l	22	0 18l	2 31s
7		2 37s	23	1 17l	3 8s
8	0 21l	2 55s	24	2 18l	3 49s
9	1 8l	3 22s	25	3 25l	4 34s
10	2 1l	3 51s	26	4 20s	5 27l
11	3 2l	4 26s	27	5 45s	6 8l
12	4 8l	5 4s	28	6 58s	6 46l
13	5 25l	5 35l	29	8 12s	7 24l
14	6 33s	6 7l	30	9 24s	8 0l
15	7 40s	6 49l	31	10 32s	8 39l
16	9 5s	7 39l			

HIGH TIDES::AUGUST.

D	Morn'g	Even'g	D	Morn'g	Even'g
1	11 33s	9 21l	17	0 13s†	10 25l
2	0 21s†	10 0l	18	0 54s†	11 20l
3	0 58s†	10 41l	19		1 27s
4	1 29s†	11 30l	20	0 13l	1 59s
5		2 4s	21	1 9l	2 57s
6	0 16l	2 6s	22	2 13s	2 51l
7	1 3l	2 27s	23	3 0s	3 27l
8	1 52l	2 48s	24	4 17s	4 9l
9	2 46l	3 14s	25	5 35s	4 53l
10	3 43s	3 53l	26	6 53s	5 39l
11	4 56s	4 30l	27	8 5s	6 25l
12	6 13s	5 13l	28	9 19s	7 21l
13	7 32s	6 6l	29	10 21s	8 14l
14	8 54s	7 0l	30	11 12s	9 6l
15	10 17s	8 17l	31	11 54s	9 52l
16	11 21s	9 23l			

ALMANAC FOR 1872.

September.
MOON'S PHASES.
New Moon, 2d. 4h. 43m. A.
First Quarter, 10d. 5h. 53m. M.
Full Moon, 16d. 8h. 54m. A.
Last Quarter, 24d. 5h. 11m. M.

October.
MOON'S PHASES.
New Moon, 2d. 7h. 20m. M.
First Quarter, 9d. 0h. 53m. A.
Full Moon, 16d. 7h. 24m. M.
Last Quarter, 24d. 0h. 43m. M.
New Moon, 31d. 9b. 18m. A.

D of M	D of W	Sun Rises h m	Sun Sets h m	Days' Length h m	Moon R & S h m	D of M	D of W	Sun Rises h m	Sun Sets h m	Days' Length h m	Moon R & S h m
1	S	5 31	6 27	12 56	4 1	1	Tu	5 57	5 41	11 44	4 54
2	Mo	5 32	6 26	12 54	5 1	2	We	5 58	5 39	11 41	5 54
3	Tu	5 33	6 24	12 51	sets	3	Th	5 59	5 38	11 39	sets
4	We	5 34	6 23	12 49	7 39	4	Fr	6 0	5 36	11 36	7 1
5	Th	5 34	6 21	12 47	8 3	5	Sa	6 0	5 35	11 35	7 33
6	Fr	5 35	6 20	12 45	8 29	6	S	6 1	5 33	11 32	8 11
7	Sa	5 36	6 18	12 42	8 58	7	Mo	6 2	5 32	11 30	8 57
8	S	5 37	6 16	12 39	9 32	8	Tu	6 3	5 31	11 28	9 52
9	Mo	5 38	6 15	12 37	10 12	9	We	6 4	5 29	11 25	10 55
10	Tu	5 38	6 13	12 35	11 2	10	Th	6 5	5 28	11 23	morn
11	We	5 39	6 12	12 33	morn	11	Fr	6 6	5 26	11 20	0 5
12	Th	5 40	6 10	12 30	0 2	12	Sa	6 7	5 25	11 18	1 20
13	Fr	5 41	6 8	12 27	1 10	13	S	6 8	5 24	11 16	2 34
14	Sa	5 42	6 7	12 25	2 24	14	Mo	6 9	5 22	11 13	3 46
15	S	5 42	6 5	12 23	3 40	15	Tu	6 10	5 21	11 11	4 57
16	Mo	5 43	6 4	12 21	4 55	16	We	6 11	5 19	11 8	rises
17	Tu	5 44	6 2	12 18	rises	17	Th	6 12	5 18	11 6	6 13
18	We	5 45	6 1	12 16	7 17	18	Fr	6 13	5 17	11 4	6 46
19	Th	5 46	5 59	12 13	7 46	19	Sa	6 14	5 15	11 1	7 21
20	Fr	5 47	5 58	12 11	8 16	20	S	6 15	5 14	10 59	8 4
21	Sa	5 48	5 56	12 8	8 50	21	Mo	6 16	5 12	10 56	8 51
22	S	5 49	5 55	12 6	9 29	22	Tu	6 17	5 11	10 54	9 43
23	Mo	5 50	5 53	12 3	10 12	23	We	6 18	5 10	10 52	10 40
24	Tu	5 51	5 52	12 1	11 1	24	Th	6 19	5 9	10 50	11 39
25	We	5 51	5 50	11 59	11 54	25	Fr	6 20	5 7	10 47	morn
26	Th	5 52	5 49	11 57	morn	26	Sa	6 21	5 6	10 45	0 39
27	Fr	5 53	5 47	11 54	0 51	27	S	6 22	5 5	10 43	1 39
28	Sa	5 54	5 45	11 51	1 50	28	Mo	6 23	5 4	10 41	2 39
29	S	5 55	5 44	11 49	2 51	29	Tu	6 24	5 3	10 39	3 40
30	Mo	5 56	5 42	11 46	3 53	30	We	6 25	5 2	10 37	4 42
						31	Th	6 26	5 1	10 35	5 46

HIGH TIDES :: SEPTEMBER.

D	Morn'g	Even'g	D	Morn'g	Even'g
1	0 26a†	10 37l	17		0 39a
2	0 51a†	11 25l	18	0 15l	1 5a
3		1 5a	19	0 51a	1 36l
4	0 13l	1 9a	20	1 56a	2 2l
5	1 0l	1 28a	21	2 52a	2 30l
6	1 42a	1 52l	22	3 56a	3 11l
7	2 36a	2 10l	23	5 11a	4 2l
8	3 40a	2 40l	24	6 28a	4 53l
9	4 57a	3 31l	25	7 47a	5 51l
10	6 19a	4 25l	26	8 51a	6 52l
11	7 43a	5 43l	27	9 50a	7 53l
12	8 59a	7 1l	28	10 41a	8 45l
13	10 10a	8 22l	29	11 19a	9 34l
14	11 5a	9 31l	30	11 48a	10 22l
15	11 40a	10 35l			
16	0 22a†	10 32l			

HIGH TIDES :: OCTOBER.

D	Morn'g	Even'g	D	Morn'g	Even'g
1	0 12a†	11 6l	17	0 29a	0 14l
2	0 30a†	11 57l	18	1 4a	0 36l
3		1 11l	19	2 2a	0 59l
4	0 38a	0 48l	20	2 50a	1 29l
5	1 31a	1 52a	21	3 55a	2 8l
6	2 28a	1 28l	22	5 2a	3 10l
7	3 34a	2 8l	23	6 10a	4 17l
8	4 50a	2 56l	24	7 15a	5 23l
9	6 20a	4 3l	25	8 11a	6 27l
10	7 40a	5 42l	26	9 1a	7 31l
11	8 51a	7 3l	27	9 45a	8 31l
12	9 55a	8 21l	28	10 21a	9 25l
13	10 44a	9 30l	29	10 49a	10 17l
14	11 20a	10 30l	30	11 31l	10 58a
15	11 48a	11 24l	31	11 40l	11 48a
16		0 11a			

ALMANAC FOR 1872.

November.
MOON'S PHASES.
First Quarter, 7d. 7h. 41m. A.
Full Moon, 14d. 8h. 58m. A.
Last Quarter, 22d. 9h. 35m. A.
New Moon, 30d. 10h. 24m. M.

December.
MOON'S PHASES.
First Quarter, 7d. 3h. 26m. M.
Full Moon, 14d. 1h. 34m. A.
Last Quarter, 22d. 6h. 1m. A.
New Moon, 29d. 10h. 26m. A.

D of M	D of W	Sun Rises h m	Sun Sets h m	Days' Length h m	Moon R & S h m	D of M	D of W	Sun Rises h m	Sun Sets h m	Days' Length h m	Moon R & S h m
1	Fr	6 27	5 0	10 33	sets	1	☉	6 58	4 41	9 43	sets
2	Sa	6 28	4 59	10 31	6 8	2	Mo	6 59	4 41	9 42	6 37
3	☉	6 29	4 58	10 29	6 53	3	Tu	7 0	4 41	9 41	7 46
4	Mo	6 30	4 57	10 27	7 46	4	We	7 1	4 41	9 40	9 0
5	Tu	6 31	4 56	10 25	8 48	5	Th	7 2	4 41	9 40	10 12
6	We	6 32	4 55	10 23	9 57	6	Fr	7 3	4 41	9 38	11 26
7	Th	6 33	4 54	10 21	11 11	7	Sa	7 4	4 41	9 37	morn
8	Fr	6 34	4 53	10 19	morn	8	☉	7 5	4 41	9 36	0 35
9	Sa	6 36	4 53	10 17	0 22	9	Mo	7 5	4 42	9 36	1 42
10	☉	6 37	4 52	10 15	1 34	10	Tu	7 6	4 42	9 36	2 48
11	Mo	6 38	4 51	10 13	2 48	11	We	7 7	4 42	9 35	3 53
12	Tu	6 39	4 50	10 11	3 51	12	Th	7 8	4 43	9 35	4 59
13	We	6 40	4 49	10 9	4 57	13	Fr	7 8	4 43	9 35	6 2
14	Th	6 41	4 48	10 6	6 4	14	Sa	7 9	4 43	9 34	7 5
15	Fr	6 42	4 48	10 6	rises	15	☉	7 9	4 44	9 34	rises
16	Sa	6 43	4 47	10 4	5 57	16	Mo	7 10	4 44	9 34	6 17
17	☉	6 44	4 46	10 2	6 43	17	Tu	7 11	4 44	9 33	7 16
18	Mo	6 45	4 46	10 1	7 33	18	We	7 11	4 45	9 33	8 15
19	Tu	6 46	4 45	9 59	8 23	19	Th	7 12	4 45	9 33	9 15
20	We	6 47	4 45	9 58	9 26	20	Fr	7 12	4 46	9 33	10 14
21	Th	6 48	4 44	9 56	10 25	21	Sa	7 13	4 46	9 33	11 12
22	Fr	6 49	4 44	9 55	11 25	22	☉	7 13	4 47	9 34	morn
23	Sa	6 50	4 43	9 53	morn	23	Mo	7 14	4 47	9 34	0 11
24	☉	6 51	4 43	9 52	0 24	24	Tu	7 14	4 48	9 34	1 11
25	Mo	6 52	4 42	9 50	1 24	25	We	7 14	4 48	9 34	2 12
26	Tu	6 53	4 42	9 49	2 25	26	Th	7 15	4 49	9 34	3 18
27	We	6 54	4 42	9 48	3 27	27	Fr	7 15	4 50	9 35	4 28
28	Th	6 55	4 42	9 47	4 32	28	Sa	7 15	4 50	9 35	5 39
29	Fr	6 56	4 41	9 45	5 40	29	☉	7 16	4 51	9 35	6 49
30	Sa	6 57	4 41	9 44	6 52	30	Mo	7 16	4 51	9 35	sets
						31	Tu	7 16	4 52	9 36	6 59

HIGH TIDES :: NOVEMBER.

D	Morn'g	Even'g	D	Morn'g	Even'g
1	11 58𝑙		17	1 51s	0 29𝑙
2	0 47s	11 47𝑙•	18	2 48s	0 51𝑙
3	1 45s	0 19𝑙	19	3 45s	1 37𝑙
4	2 44s	0 50𝑙	20	4 37s	2 35𝑙•
5	3 50s	1 50𝑙	21	5 33s	3 44𝑙
6	5 4s	3 6𝑙	22	6 32s	4 49𝑙
7	6 17s	4 29𝑙	23	7 23s•	5 52𝑙
8	7 27s	5 53𝑙	24	8 4s•	6 55𝑙
9	8 25s	7 12𝑙	25	8 45s•	7 50𝑙
10	9 18s	8 28𝑙	26	0 13𝑙	0 6s
11	9 59s	9 35𝑙	27	9 48𝑙	10 4s
12	10 30s	10 34𝑙	28	10 14𝑙	11 3s
13	10 56𝑙	11 28𝑙•	29	10 37𝑙	
14	11 25𝑙		30	0 0s	10 34𝑙•
15	0 15s	11 45𝑙•			
16	1 11s	11 54𝑙•			

HIGH TIDES :: DECEMBER.

D	Morn'g	Even'g	D	Morn'g	Even'g
1	0 53s	10 59𝑙•	17	2 46s•	0 29𝑙
2	1 58s	11 58𝑙•	18	3 27s	1 16𝑙
3	2 52s	0 54𝑙	19	4 4s	2 10𝑙
4	3 45s	1 57𝑙	20	4 44s	3 15𝑙
5	4 47s	3 13𝑙	21	5 29s	4 22𝑙
6	5 53s	4 39𝑙	22	6 12s	5 27𝑙
7	6 51s	6 1𝑙	23	6 51s	6 31𝑙
8	7 38s	7 14𝑙	24	7 46𝑙	7 29s
9	8 27s	8 27𝑙	25	8 11𝑙	8 35s
10	9 1s	9 33𝑙	26	8 48𝑙	9 47s
11	9 42𝑙	10 32s	27	9 21𝑙	10 53s
12	10 9𝑙	11 35s	28	9 52𝑙	11 54s
13	10 30𝑙		29	10 26𝑙	
14	0 30s	10 51𝑙•	30	0 55s	10 55𝑙•
15	1 7𝑙•	11 7𝑙	31	1 52s	11 54𝑙•
16	2 1s	11 46𝑙•			

- Rory O'More
- Tempest
- ~~for rent~~
- Solteiro
- Chorus
- Celebrated ???
- ??? ???
- ??? ???
- Liverpool
- Exchange
- Cagley ??? the water
- ??? ???
- Flower of Edinburg
- ??? ???
- St Patrick day morning
- Irish Washerwoman
- Which ???
- Sany O Gaff
- ??? ???
- ??? Schottische
- Mahungdy
- Rockwitz

Tuesday, January 2, 1872.

Prima Donna Waltz
A Life on the Ocean [?]
Elfin Waltz
Bold Soldier Boy
Yankee Doodle
Erin's [?]
Stars of [?]
Kate Kearney Waltz
Buy a Broom "
Hungarian "
Swiss "
Polly Hopkins "
Copenhagen "
Steam Boat "

Wednesday, January 3, 1872.

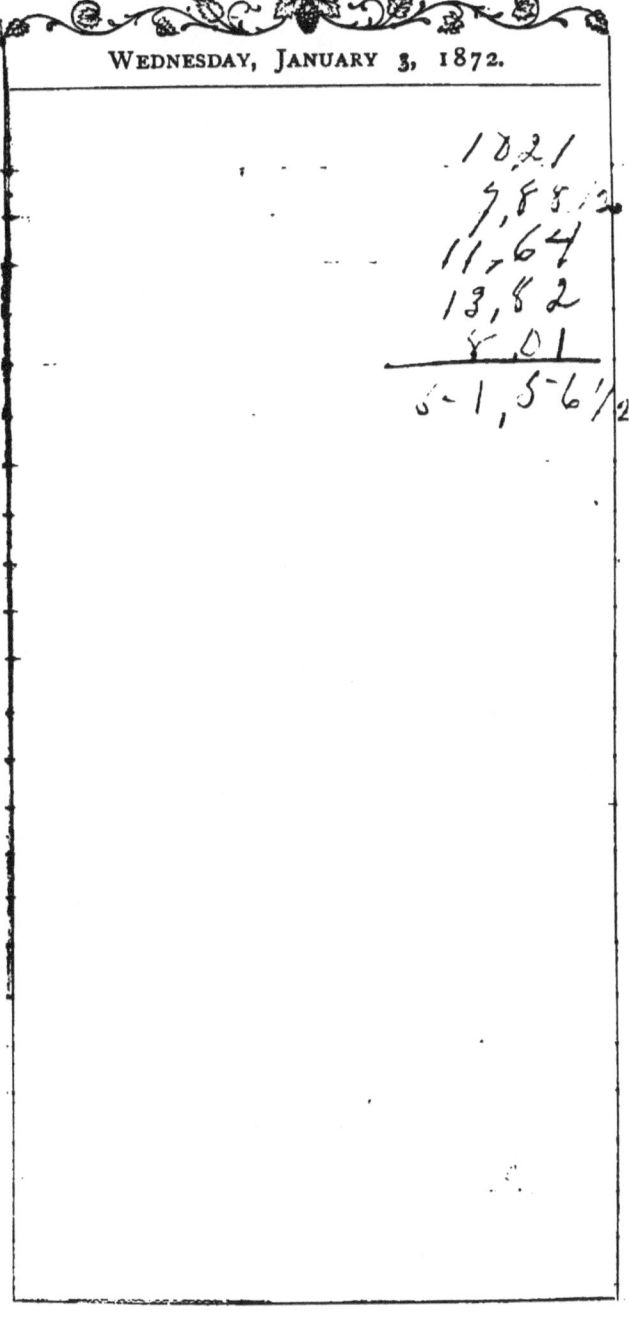

            18.21
             7.88½
           11.64
           13.82
             8.01
          51.56½

Friday, January 5, 1872.

Jan 3d. 1879
1 Mack Garrick 1 bsl
1 ton of Cane W84

To Mr Emerson
~~1 lot of Squash~~
~~and potatoes & beets~~
~~$1.00~~

James W.
Horan - G.
Benj. Bu[l]

Sunday, February 4, 1872.

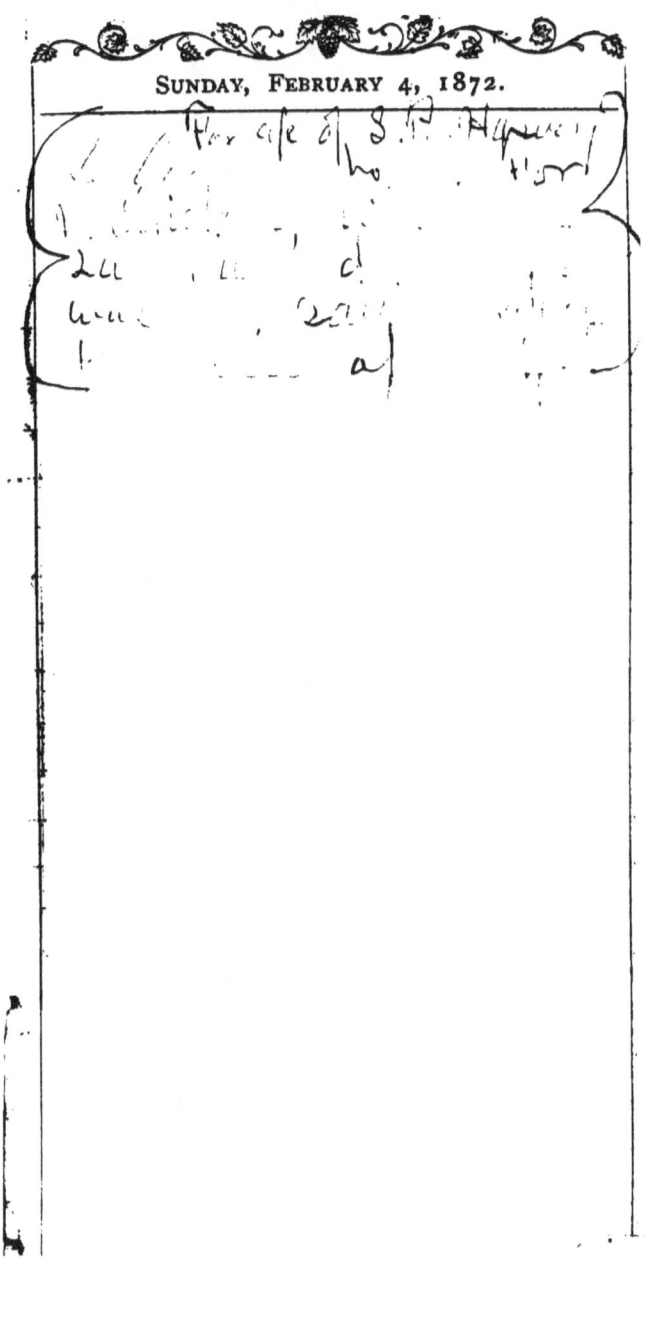

Tuesday, February 6, 1872.

Friday, February 9, 1872.

Drawing the land in
various places in front
field.
Went to Amado to get some
farming tools.

Saturday, February 10, 1872.

Hauled to Lambtin 1½ box apples to be shipped to Fisk & Shier.

Ploughed several furrows in front field, &part to let off water.

Weather dull, wind light S.E. with indications of rain.

7 o'clock P.M. weather cloudy, wind North west raining gently.

10 o'clock P.M. Weather dull and heavy, wind N.W. raining quite steady, with no signs of a cessation.

Sunday, February 11, 1872.

Went over to Louie's and Mother's. She being there to attend to Hattie in her sickness of Typhus Chorey. Went to ——

7 [?] ... R.M. Commenced raining with considerable force and dust. Sun bathes [baby?] which is said to weigh 7 lbs. 30 minutes past 7 experienced a shock of earthquake which seemed to be from North towards the South, and which is the most severe of the season.

9

MONDAY, FEBRUARY 12, 1872.

Planting hand in front
field.
Rained at [Mr Humphries?]
Went to town got [some?]
spindles, [&c.] [Home by?]
Express. which are for
my old Buggy. my
Cost [unless cheap?]
inclu[ding] $1.25.
Went over to H Sowie's
to help [barrel?] out
to attend [to?] [Pavis?], saw
Mack, said he was
going to see [Sowie?].
Returned by way of
Buchanan's [fond?] of
road very bad and
almost impassable.
Weather clear, wind
West with some in-
dications of rain.
7 o clock. [Very beauti-]
ful evening. stars shin-
ing bright and [bids fair for]
good weather.

TUESDAY, FEBRUARY 13, 1872.

Wrote a letter to Frank
and ... to ... ...
... ... between
... ... towell
but was disappointed as
as it was ... ...
to the ... ...
was ... ...
to ... ... Morning
... ... and ...
... ... at
... ...
... ...
... ... a steamer
...
... ...
...
attack ... ...
... cloudy, wind
...
... ... but
...

Wednesday, February 14, 1872.

Draining land with spade and with Horses very wet, and disagreeable [illegible].
Sawing wood and doing sundry things after [dinner].
I received no paper to day could not ascertain the cause.
Weather cloudy, wind West with [indications] of rain, although no [illegible], [indeed] a rain is [wanted] [illegible] to have it [illegible] [illegible], that being the general cause to bring on rain.

[illegible handwritten text]

Friday, February 16, 1872.

Cut [...] wood at the [...]
[...] a part of the
[...]
[...] for the
Mail. Sam McElker-
[...] had a conver-
sation on [...]
[...] Alabama Claims
[...] time on the
[...] he was speaking
of the work he [...] at
[...]
[...] it [...]
[...]
[...] wind
8 E with indications
of a long storm.
Received [...]
from St.
[...]

Saturday, February 17, 1872.

[Handwritten entry, largely illegible]

Went out in the [...] and [...] Father [...] away from the [...] in the afternoon, and [...] by Charles City. Got some [...] Got the 2 puppies out [...] and they are [...] the [...] size and shape.
With own Helen and of Laura [...].
O Weather [...] right showers. Wind N.W.

that they at
and go to
stated I
you to a

[illegible handwritten notes]

dug...... allenes.
Will I have to
done two books, and
to the ? ??? di...
Robert ?????,
Another ???? ??
?? ???? of the ??
???? has at least,
??. Sun ???????
Dutch ???? ?????.
Bath, a? ? ?????,
Weather, cloudy in
morning which ????
appears towards —
Wind ?????? ????

[illegible] [illegible] pleasing as
if the [illegible] Commi-
-ssion bear animals.
Went over to [illegible] Fields,
and from [illegible]
[illegible] to [illegible]. Rec-
-eived a letter from
Aunt Emma.
Mack was [illegible] in the
evening and slept all
night.
Weather cloudy, and frequent
[illegible] indications of rain.
[illegible] in the afternoon
Commenced raining
with a storm SW wind
Went to [illegible] [illegible]

SATURDAY, FEBRUARY 24, 1872.

Went to town [...] [...]
received a [...] [...]
[...] had [...] Com-
[...] with [...]
[...] Concerning the
present state of [...]
and our [...]
C[...]
[...]
[...]
[...] the Creek
to all the [...] [...]
as [...] at present
occasioned by recent
rains.
Weather cloudy, and
raining most the time
during the day.
Ponds over flowed in
many places.
Bought 50$ worth Postage
Stamps.

Went to [...] to [...]
Mail, and to take [...]
[...] up [...] &c.
drawing board after my
turn which [...] at
easy job as account
[...] out state at
[...] [...]
Saw [Mr?] [...] Catherine
[...] [...] [...] [...]
[...] [...]
[...] [...] it
[...] [...]
Wrote a [...] [...]
and one to S. Thompson
received one [...]
Wind west [...]
[...] [...]
Sky clear.

Tuesday, February 27, 1872.

This day was spent in various ways.
Had a bath and early breakfast and which was a dilly, at a great rate keeping water up. A few down the road.
Weather cloudy, and wind SE, with indications of rain, which later did come late in the day, and which came at a fearful rate causing the [overflow], and [making the land] [wet].

Wrote two letters, one to Uncle Silvester and one to [____].

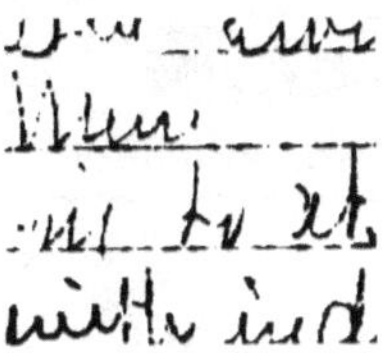

illegible handwritten notes

Thursday, February 29, 1872.

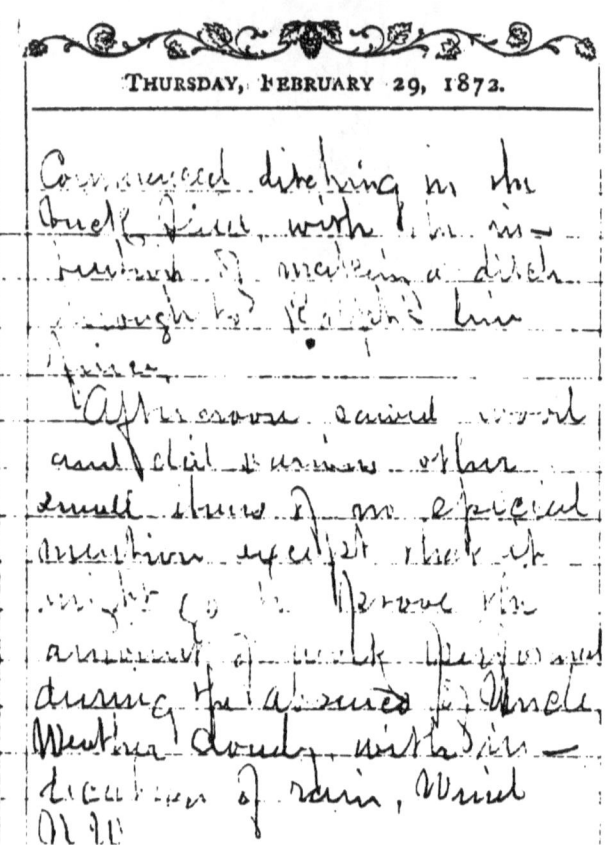

Commenced ditching in the buck field, with the intention of making a ditch enough to [?] the line fence.

Afternoon sawed wood and did various other small chores of no special mention except that it might be to [?] the amount of work performed during the absence of Uncle. Weather cloudy with indications of rain, Wind N.W.

much when seen
together as these
[?] must of
[?] of work [?]

word and
Chorus.
Church with

Went to Kansas City to
take 12 Bus Supplies, and
to ship down to the City.
After noon hauled down
to J. McKown's Black
Smith Shop 2084
Barley to be ground in —
" full
Weather cloudy, wind
West most of the day,
When late in the
day it changed to
S.E. and from which
course there seems
to be some serious ill

Tuesday, March 5, 1872

This day went to Aivarads,
with one load of Barley
4 ch ground.
Sold 1216 to Smithers
Joe $1.50.
Weather Cloudy and
raining, wind S.E.

Wednesday, March 6, 1872.

Went out in the park
with runaway Catherine
[...] [...] the
[...]
And after [...]
went to town to get
my watch and to see
about the great Berlin
[...] mail.
After which we went
down [...] in
[...]
[...]
till nearly dark and just
[...]
[...]
[...] came with
[...] and
[...] about [...]

Thursday, March 7, 1872.

This day was spent in
various ways. I
[illegible] at [illegible] [illegible]
and afternoon com-
menced [illegible] the
[illegible] Sunday in the
evening. I
worked on [illegible]
[illegible] a [illegible]
[illegible] not [illegible] [illegible]
[illegible] [illegible] [illegible]
[illegible] [illegible]

Friday, March 8, 1872

Chopping in the front field, spent evening
over things that I
will have to leave
until I come home.
Received Weekly news
on good Republican
papers. Wind strong
from the west.

Saturday, March 9, 1872.

A badly day, a man
who is dying did not
perish but went
to hospital and got
a couple of meals
for himself.
Weather dull, and
there is sign of
rain.
Wind west.

Sunday, March 10, 1872.

This day was spent in
ordinary ways, the occurences
incidents to discussion
and none of which
would require special
mention.
Weather cloudy and
raining.

MONDAY, MARCH. 11, 1872.

[illegible] to Alvarado,
to get the Mail and
see how the spirit
[illegible] high [illegible]
[illegible] in the people
[illegible] the
[illegible].

[illegible]
[illegible] &c.
Weather cloudy and
[illegible].

Wednesday, March 13, 1872.

[handwritten entry, largely illegible]

Thursday, March 14, 1872.

Friday, March 15, 1872.

Saturday, March 16, 1872.

Sunday, March 17, 1872.

Wednesday, March 20, 1872.

THURSDAY, MARCH 21, 1872.

Sunday, March 24, 1872.

Monday, March 25, 1872.

Wednesday, March 27, 1872.

TUESDAY, APRIL 2, 1872.

```
      16
      12
     ───
      3 2
       6
     ┌───
  15)1 9 2 1 3
     1 5
     ─────
       4 2
       4 5
```

```
         16
         15
        ───
         8 0
         ┌─
         4 8
     12)2 4 0
        ─────
         2 0
```

```
         12
         15
        ───
         6 1
         12
     12)1 4 0
        ─────
         7 0
```

J Martin Com-
menced work with
us with one team
Commencing at morning
to folwogh.

Saturday, April 6, 1872.

Mr Lewridge was away to day, and Duncan took his run to Thurrow.

Monday, April 8, 1872.

Wednesday, April 10, 1872.

Thursday, April 11, 1872.

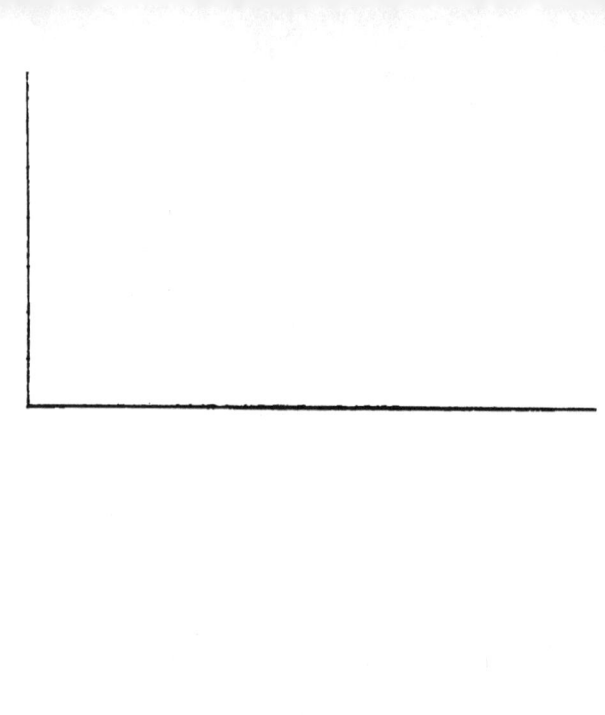

Tuesday, April 16, 1872.

WEDNESDAY, APRIL 17, 1872.

Thursday, April 18, 1872.

FRIDAY, APRIL 19, 1872.

Saturday, April 20, 1872.

Tuesday, April 23, 1872.

WEDNESDAY, APRIL 24, 1872.

Friday, April 26, 1872.

MONDAY, APRIL 29, 1872.

Sunday, May 5, 1872.

$$\frac{400}{9}$$

$$5\overline{)3600}$$

$$22\overline{)3600}(163$$
$$\underline{22}$$
$$140$$
$$\underline{132}$$
$$80$$
$$66$$

$$\begin{array}{r}27,5\overline{)3600}\,(128\\275\\\hline 850\\550\\\hline 200\end{array}$$

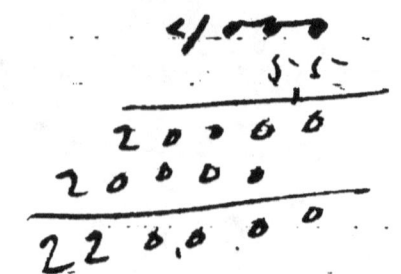

```
    160 ) 2 2 0 ( 1
          1 6 0
          ─────
            1 0
```

Wednesday, May 8, 1872.

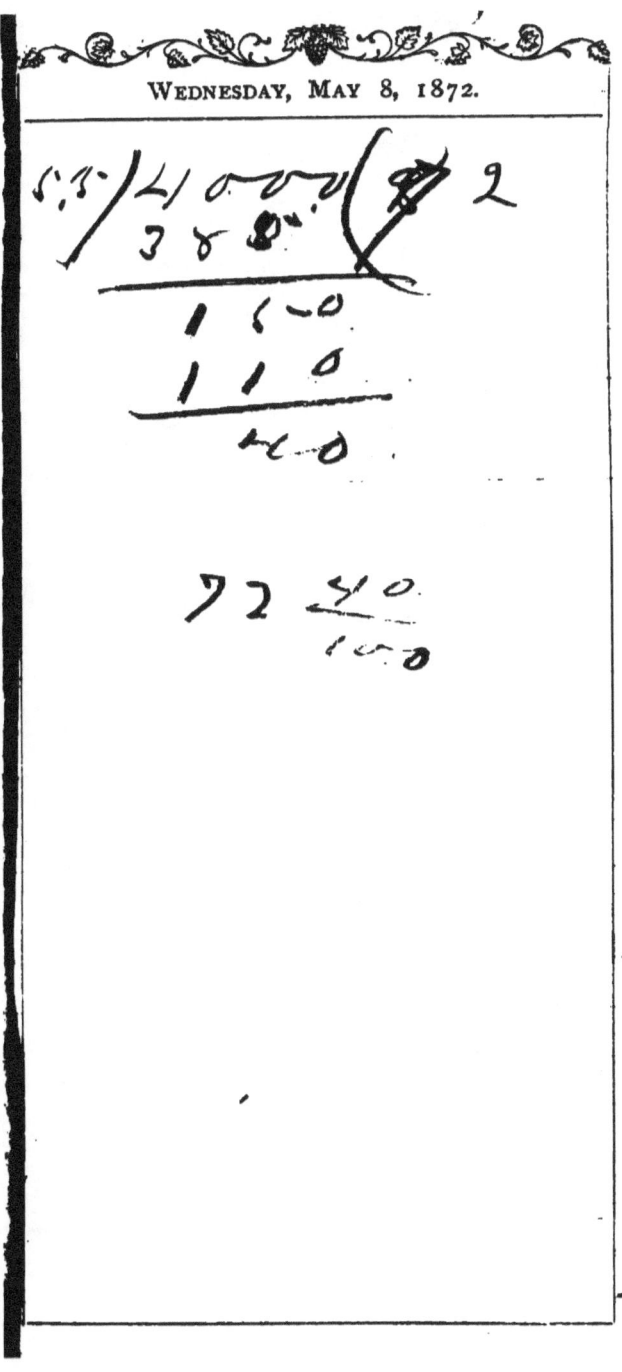

Thursday, May 9, 1872.

65.40

$$30.25 \overline{\smash{\big)}\,36000}\,(11$$
$$\underline{3025}$$
$$5750$$
$$\underline{3025}$$
$$2725$$

Friday, May 10, 1872.

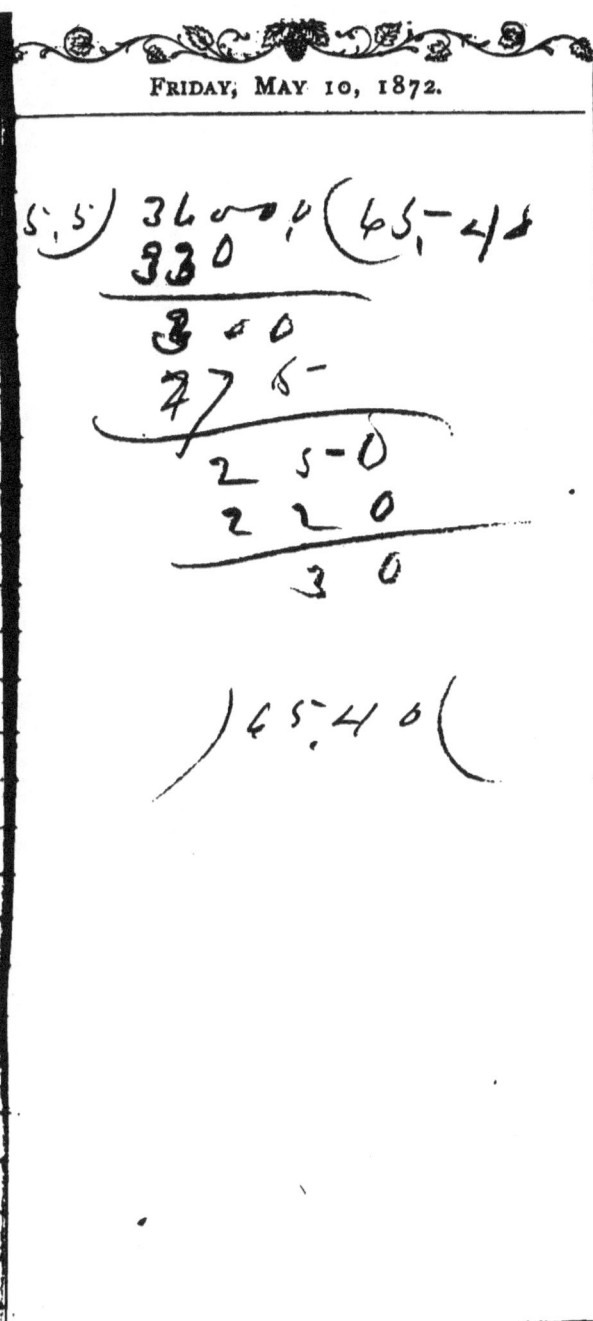

Sunday, May 12, 1872.

Monday, May 13, 1872.

TUESDAY, MAY 14, 1872.

WEDNESDAY, MAY 15, 1872.

Thursday, May 16, 1872.

Friday, May 17, 1872.

Saturday, May 18, 1872.

Sunday, May 19, 1874

John Carlyon
to cash
July 4th   15 7/
                $4.5

MONDAY, MAY 20, 1872/4

Case argued
commenced
at Park Des Moines
May 20 in 1874

Tuesday, May 21, 1872.

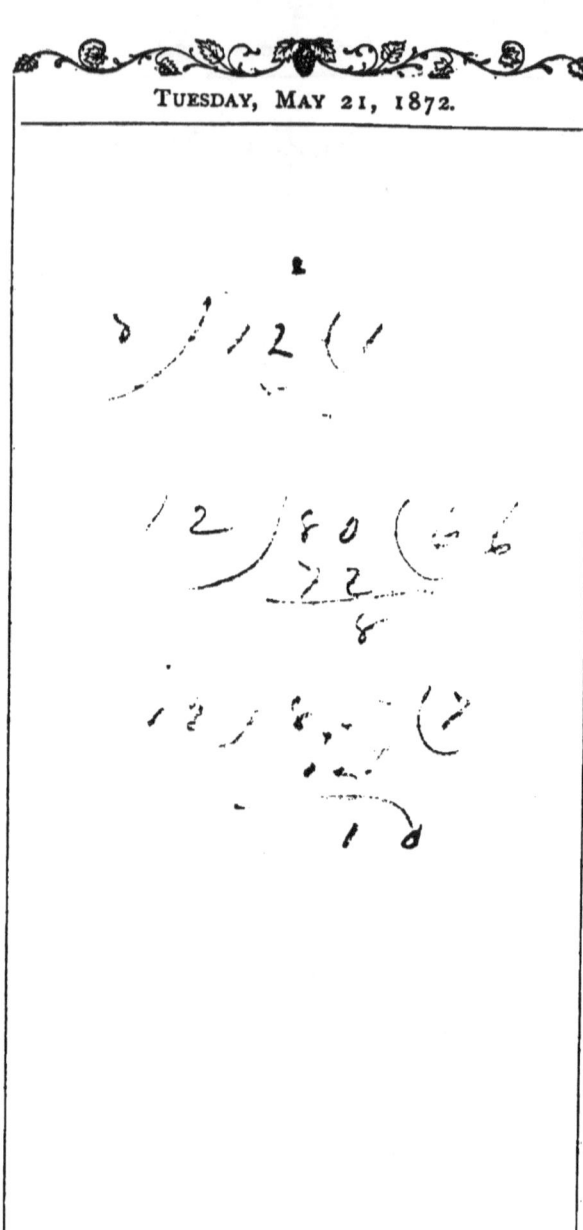

Wednesday, May 22, 1872.

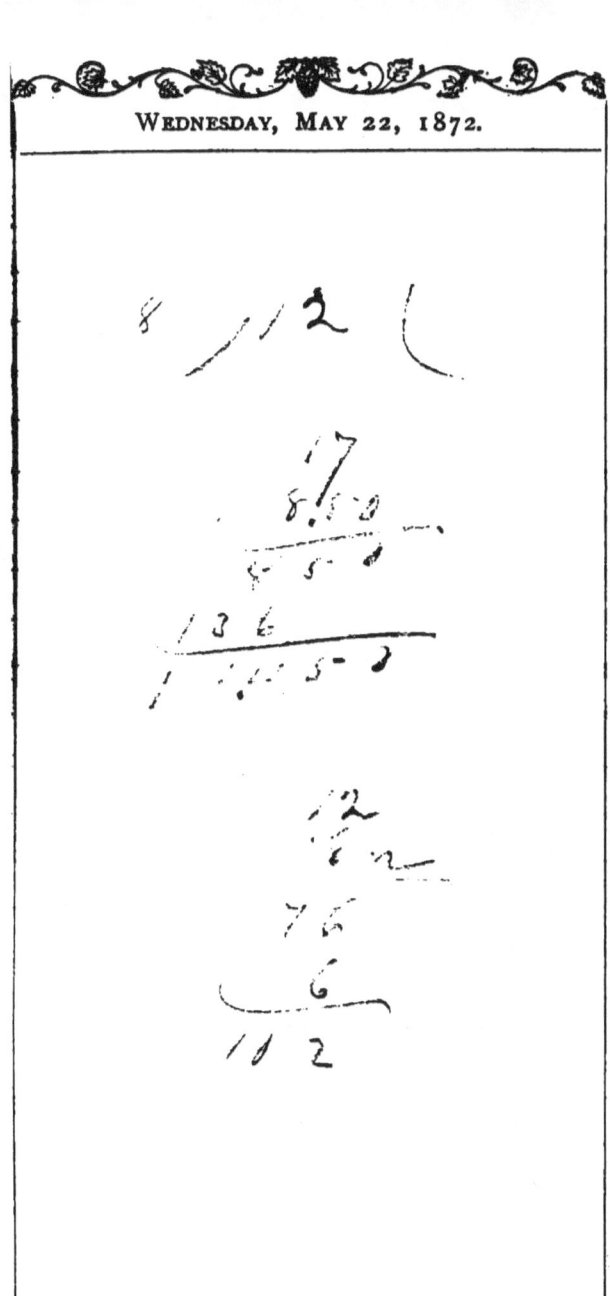

Friday, May 24, 1872.

Saturday, May 25, 1872.

Monday, May 27, 1872.

Tuesday, May 28, 1872.

THURSDAY, MAY 30, 1872.

Friday, May 31, 1872.

Saturday, June 1, 1872.

SUNDAY, JUNE 2, 1872.

Monday, June 3, 1872.

Tuesday, June 4, 1872.

Wednesday, June 5, 1872.

Thursday, June 6, 1872.

Friday, June 7, 1872.

1878

Malcom Garrick
Commenced work
for S. P. Harvey
April 2nd - with two
horses

2d " "   " "   1
4th "   1
5th "   1
6   1
8   1
9   1
10   1
11   1
12   1
13   1
14   1
15   ½
16   1
17   1
1   1
2   1
3   1
4   1
5   1
6   1
7   1
8   1
9   1

Saturday, June 8, 1872.

Stolen sent a man
and 4 horses.
Commenced work
the afternoon of
the 8 of April = 1 07
worked   9 of April
  "   10   "   "
  "   11   "   "
  "   12   "   "
            13   "
" half day 1?   "
Man, 1 day 19 team
            21
            2 ?
            2 ?
            2 4
            2 5
            2 6
            2 8
            ━━━━
            2 ?   ━━━
            3 0   1/2

Sunday, June 9, 1872.

Peter Campbell 62
by one man and 2
horses, the 9th 2
April afternoon —
and worked half 1½
day the 62 April   1
all day   "   "   "   1
  "   2 "   "   1
  "   3 "   "   1
         2 1
         2 2
         6
         8
        10
        11

Monday, June 10, 1872.

Tuesday, June 11, 1872. 1878

Emerson Sent 2 men and 4 horses, commenced work the 10th of April — 1
" 11   "   "   1
" 12   "   "   1
" 13   "   "   ½
" 17   "   "

19   1
21   1
22   1
23   1
24   1
25   1

Liana and man left 2 p.m   1
27   one team   1
28   " "   1
30   " "   1
May 2nd   " "   1
" 3   1
" 4   1
" 6   1
" 7   1
" 8   1

WEDNESDAY, JUNE 12, 1872.

THURSDAY, JUNE 13, 1872.

FRIDAY, JUNE 14, 1872.

Saturday, June 15, 1872.

Sunday, June 16, 1872.

Monday, June 17, 1872.

TUESDAY, JUNE 18, 1872.

Wednesday, June 19, 1872.

THURSDAY, JUNE 20, 1872.

Friday, June 21, 1872.

Sunday, June 23, 1872.

George Williams
Commenced
Work for Harvey
June 24. 1874

Tuesday, June 25, 1874

George Williams
to Cash
July 4 $5 00
"   16   25 00
Aug   20

Nov 5 to Cash 20
"   1 to Boys   50
Dec
Nov 25 to cash 20
January 1 to Boots 5
"   " 21 to Cash 20
                    1
1 Knife   1 25
1 "   75
   "Socks   1 00
July 5   20 00
                 139 50
Sept 3 Paid   290 50
     3           $429 00

WEDNESDAY, JUNE 26, 1872.

Thursday, June 27, 1875

September 3. 1875
George Williams
Commenced
Work for Harvey

Friday, June 28, 1872.

Saturday, June 29, 1872.

Dec 24th 1875
George Williams

24	to cash	$20.00
April 8 1876	to cash	60.00
July 8	to cash	20.00
	taxes	2.00
	socks	50
Sept 23	to cash	20.00
	stockings	1.00
1878		40
	cash tax	4.00
		40

1877

	Poll tax	2.00
	to cash	10.00
July	socks	5.00
Aug 5	cash	20.00
	50	4.0
Dec		10
		20

275.90

Sunday, June 30, 1872.

January 14 1876

Mc Carrick
to Paul ks Corn
14   lbs 5.33
Mc Carrick 1877
to Cash $53.00

TUESDAY, JULY 2, 1872.

WEDNESDAY, JULY 3, 1872.

~~Mr Carrick~~

~~Sunday~~

Dec to Paid
to Cash

1875
$36.00

Thursday, July 4, 1872.

Saturday, July 6, 1872.

W. T. Ralph 1876
SUNDAY, JULY 1872.

Peter By Woske
... 5
5 by 11 Days Worke $11.00

Monday, July 8, 1872.

Tuesday, July 9, 1872.

Wednesday, July 3, 1872

Green ____

to Cash	$10
to "	10
to Boots	5
"	5
" to Cash	20

Gen. Harvey

May 9th 1877
Cash $1.83

Friday, July 12, 1872.

George Willard
March 24, 1875

24 to Cash $20

March 4 1878

George Williams

Commenced Work
For Harvey

TUESDAY, JULY 16, 1872.

Thursday, July 18, 1872.

Friday, July 19, 1872.

Monday, July 22, 1872.

Tuesday, July 23, 1872.

THURSDAY, JULY 25, 1872.

FRIDAY, JULY 26, 1872.

Hob or Nob,
Pop goes the weasel,
already over the water.

Rochester Schottische

Irish washer woman.
White Cockade,
On the road to
Boston.

Ricketts Hornpipe
Liverpool Hornpipe
Durange Hornpipe,

Wednesday, July 31, 1872.

Sunday, September 22, 1872.

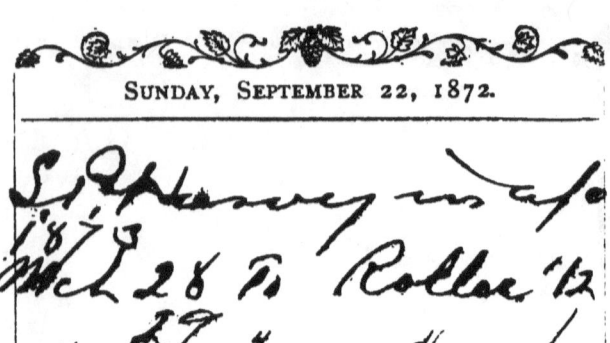

Monday, September 23, 1872.

with us morning
day
"

Tuesday, September 24, 1872.

WEDNESDAY, SEPTEMBER 25, 1872.

with Montrose
[illegible]

Thursday, September 26, 1872.

Friday, September 27, 1872.

SATURDAY, SEPTEMBER   1873

S R Harvey Esq

1873
Oct 21 " Th. N Jones
 " 22 "   1.   "
 " 24 "   4.   "
 " 25 "   1.   "
 " 26 "   4   4

for S R Harvey

Sunday, September 29, 1872.

MONDAY, SEPTEMBER 30, 1872.

J. P. Harvey in a/c with
1873
Mch 14 -To Duncan and
 "   "   " M Currick
 " 15   "   "   "
 "   "   " Duncan
 " 17   " M Currick
 "   "   " Duncan
 " 18   " M Currick
 " 19   " Duncan
 " 20   " M Currick

Tuesday, October 1, 1872.

M Carrick.

2 Horses & dray
2 " 1 "
2 " 1 "
2 " 1 "
2 " 1 "
2 " 1 "
2 " 1 "
2 " 1 "
2 " 1 "
2 " 1 "
2 " 1 "
2 " ½ "
2 " ½ "

WEDNESDAY, OCTOBER 2, 1872.

S. P. Harvey in a/c
1873
March 18 To 2 Men
" 19 " 2 "
" 20 " 2 "
" 21 " 2 "
" 22 " 2 "
" 24 " 2 "
" 25 " 2 "

Thursday, October 3, 1872.

Friday, October 4, 1872.

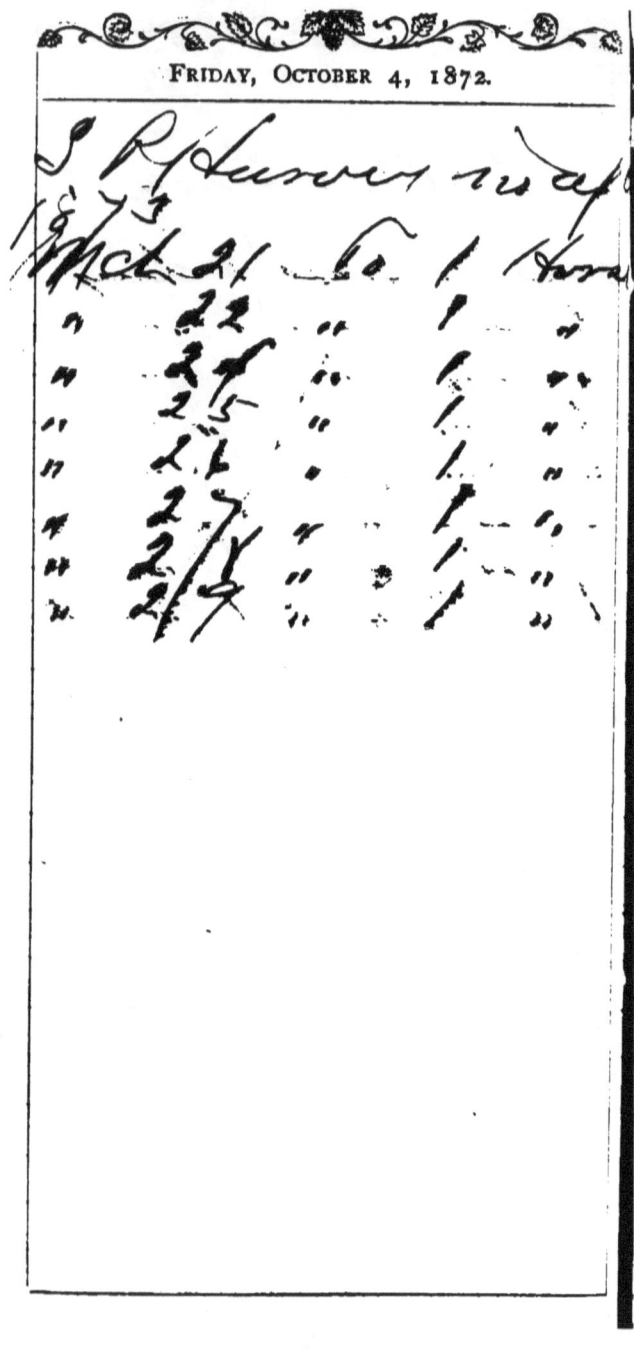

Saturday, October 5, 1872.

with M Currie
½ day ploughing

Sunday, October 6, 1872.

S. P. Harvey m a/c
1872
Oct 20th   ½ days work
 "   21 "   1   "   "
 "   23 "   1   "   "
 "   24 "   1   "   "
 "   25 "   1   "   "
 "   26 "   1   "   "
 "   27 "   1   "   "
 "   28 "   1   "   "
 "   29 "   1   "   "

Monday, October 7, 1872.

with McFarland.

TUESDAY, OCTOBER 8, 1872.

J. K. Harvey … C

1873

Mch 22	To	J. Emery	4	[illegible]
" 24	"	J. Emery	4	"
" 25	"	"	"	4	"
" 26	"	"	"	4	"
" 27	"	"	"	4	"

WEDNESDAY, OCTOBER 9, 1872.

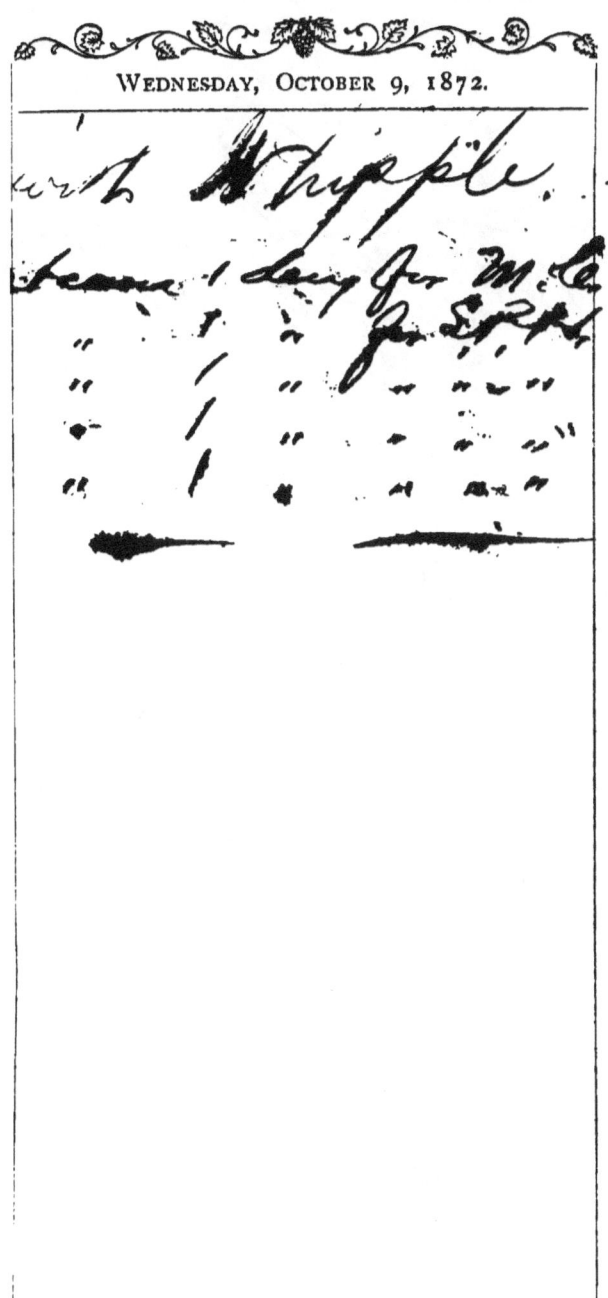

Thursday, October 10, 1872.

1873
Commenced sow-
ing Barly on the
9 [?] Wheat in
Buck Feild.

Saturday, October 12, 1872.

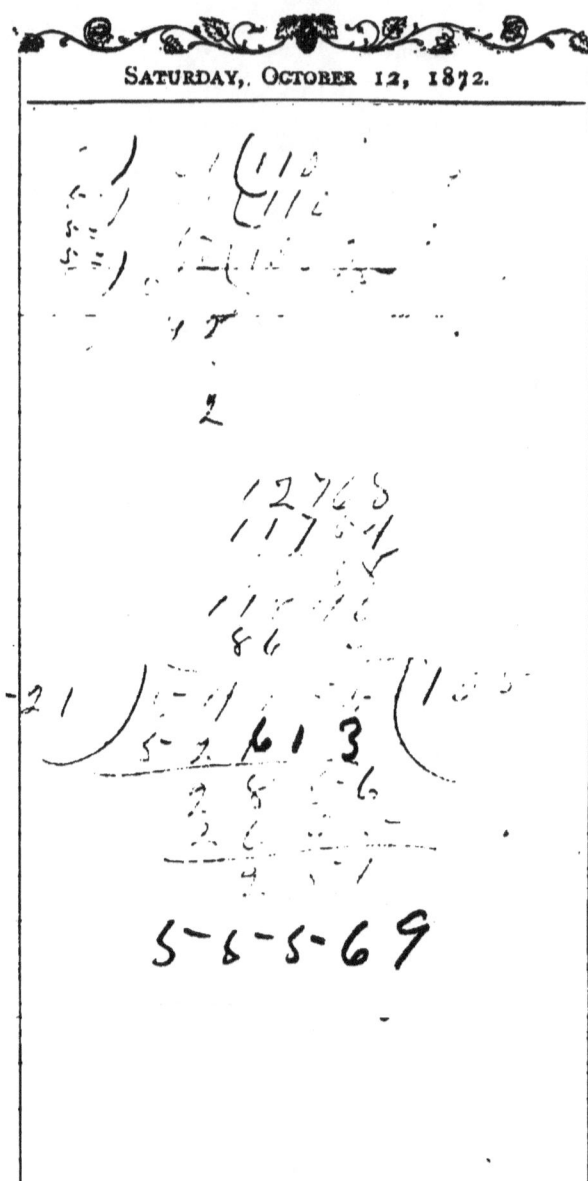

5-5-5-6 9

Monday, October 14, 1872.

[handwritten ledger entries, largely illegible]

5 =   5 = 5.2
5 =   5 = 49
5 =   = 5.1
        = 5.1
5 = 5.19   = 5.16
5 = 5   5 = 5.30
            5 = 5.26
    5.2   5
5 = 2.2   5
5 =   = .6
5 = 5.1   = 5.2
5 = 11   = 5.19
5
5 = 5.1
            5 =
5 =   = 5.21
5 = 5.5
5 =
5 = 5.1   5 =   .5
5   9 —
            8 1 5 - 0
            5 = 5.0 8
            9 1 5 - 8
1 = 1 0 5   1 = 1 0 5 —
1 1 9 5 - 1   9 2 6 3

Tuesday, October 15, 1872.

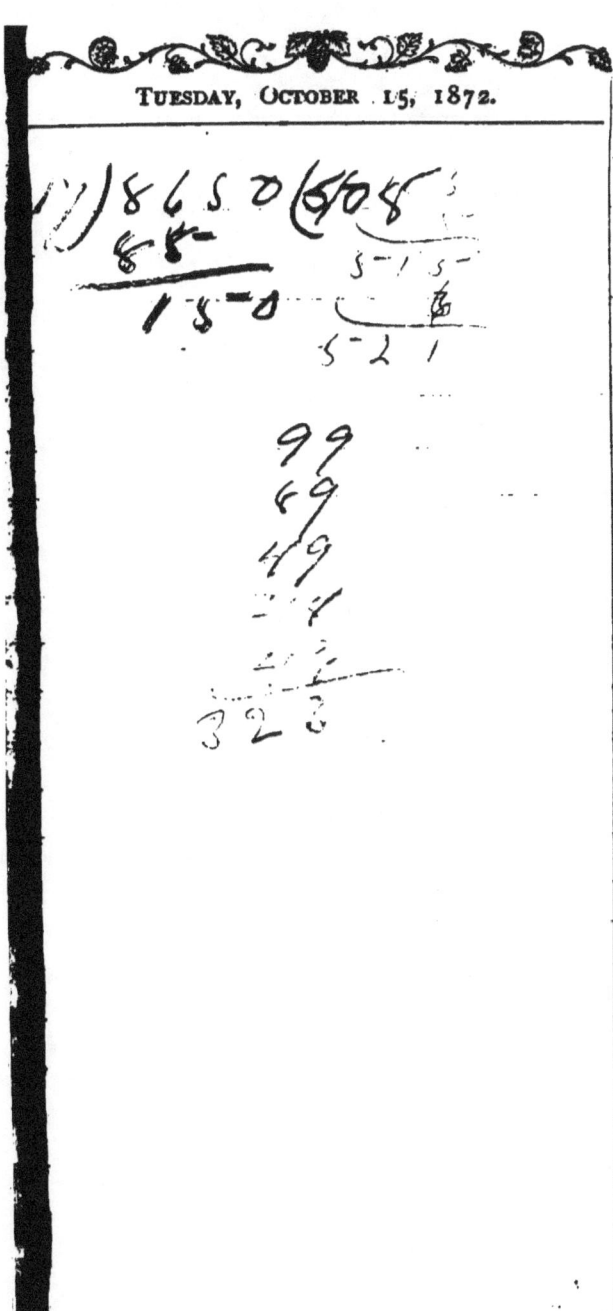

WEDNESDAY, OCTOBER 16, 1872.

490
37
45-3

```
      9263
      11981
      9938
      11757
  -27)12768
       5567 4(105
       5 7
       2974
       263 5
       339
```

Saturday, October 19, 1872.

TUESDAY, OCTOBER 22, 1872.

Wednesday, October 23, 1872.

October 7 & 8 1873
Radu Smarte

Friday, October 25, 1872.

Sunday, October 27, 1872.

Monday, October 28, 1872.

Tuesday, October 29, 1872.

Wednesday, October 30, 1872.

Thursday, October 31, 1872.

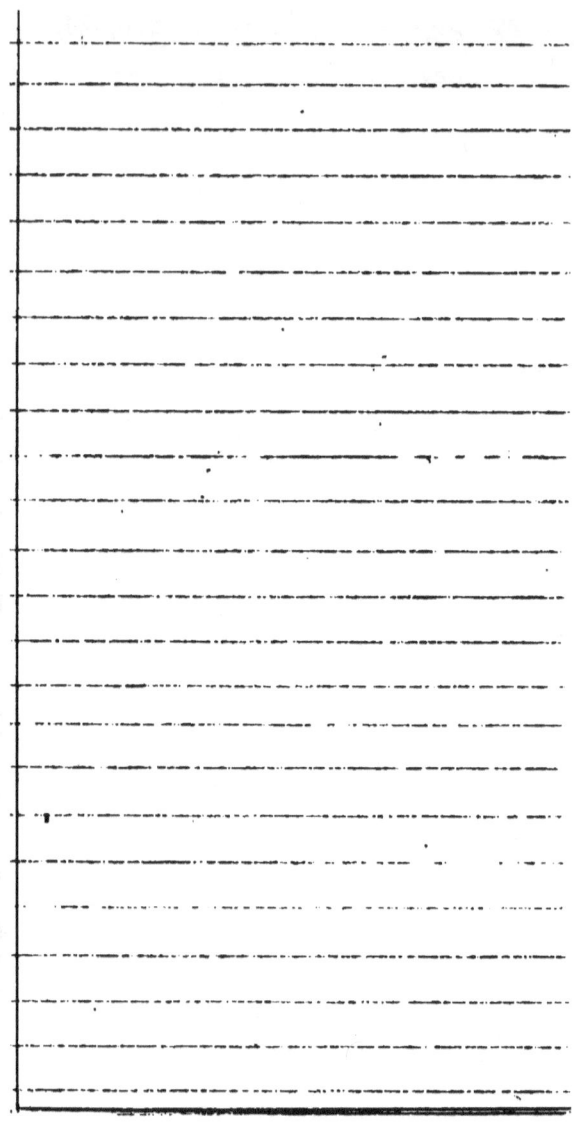

SATURDAY, NOVEMBER 2, 1872.

Monday, November 4, 1872.

Tuesday, November 5, 1872.

Thursday, November 7, 1872.

Friday, November 8, 1872.

SATURDAY, NOVEMBER 9, 1872.

Sunday, November 10, 1872.

Monday, November 11, 1872.

Tuesday, November 12, 1872.

WEDNESDAY, NOVEMBER 13, 1872.

Friday, November 15, 1872.

SATURDAY, NOVEMBER 16, 1872.

Sunday, November 17, 1872.

Monday, November 18, 1872.

Tuesday, November 19, 1872.

WEDNESDAY, NOVEMBER 20, 1872.

Thursday, November 21, 1872.

Saturday, November 23, 1872.

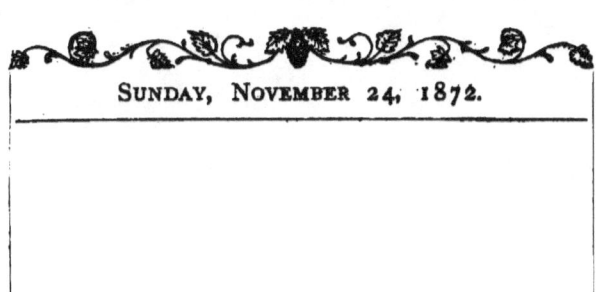

Sunday, November 24, 1872.

MONDAY, NOVEMBER 25, 1872.

Tuesday, November 26, 1872.

WEDNESDAY, NOVEMBER 27, 1872.

Thursday, November 28, 1872.

Friday, November 29, 1872.

Saturday, November 30, 1872.

Sunday, December 1, 1872.

MONDAY, DECEMBER 2, 1872.

TUESDAY, DECEMBER 3, 1872.

Wednesday, December 4, 1872

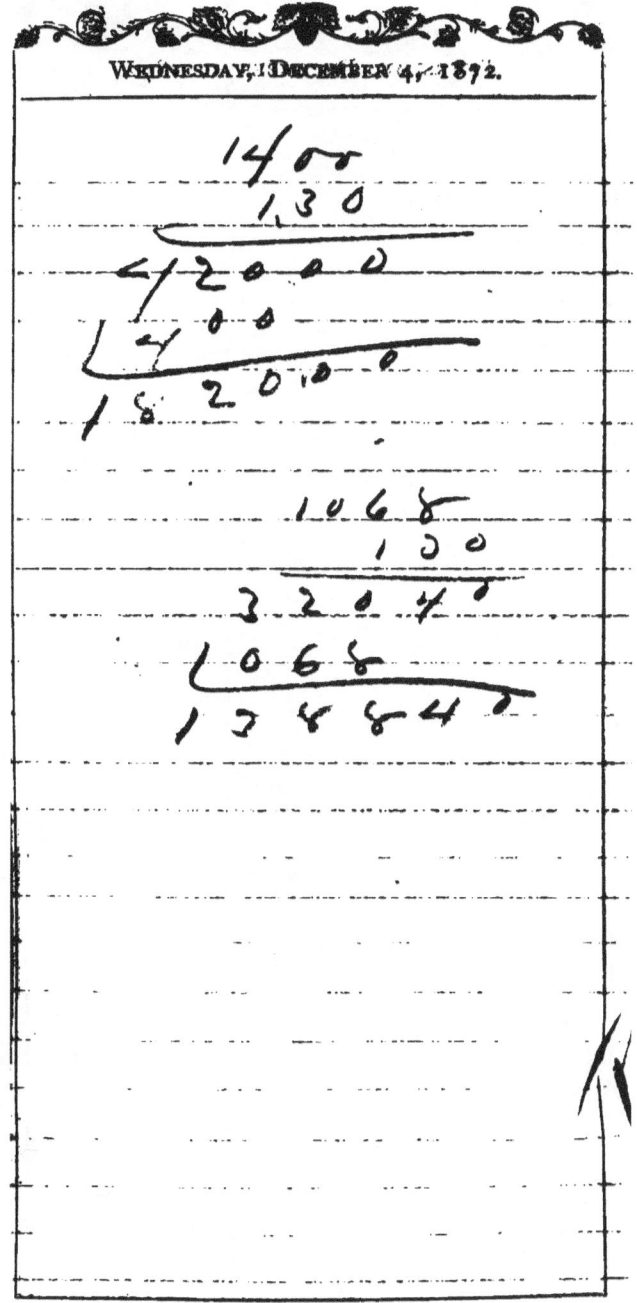

Thursday, December 5, 1872.

Friday, December 6, 1872.

SATURDAY, DECEMBER 7, 1872.

SUNDAY, DECEMBER 8, 1872.

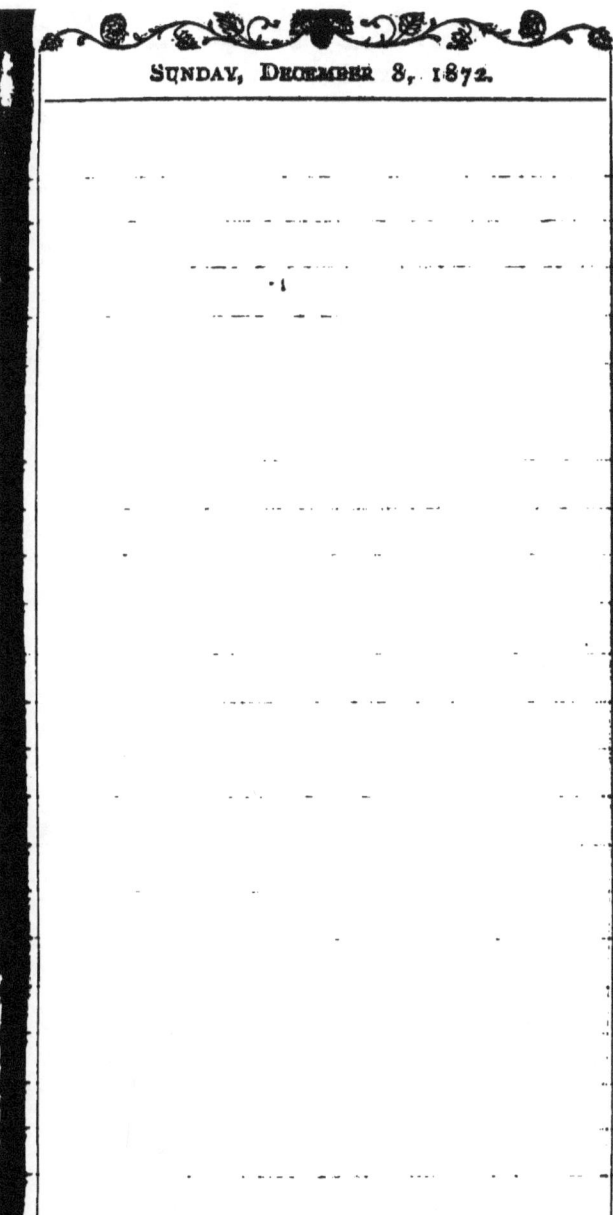

MONDAY, DECEMBER 9, 1872.

Tuesday, December 10, 1872.

Went over to Hull in Company with Mr Nolan about his bailey

Wednesday, December 11, 1872.

Thursday, December 12, 1872.

FRIDAY, DECEMBER 13, 1872.

Saturday, December 14, 1872.

SUNDAY, DECEMBER 15, 1872.

Monday, December 16, 1872

Tuesday, December 17, 1872.

WEDNESDAY, DECEMBER 18, 1872.

THURSDAY, DECEMBER 19, 1872

FRIDAY, DECEMBER 20, 1872.

Sunday, December 22, 1872.

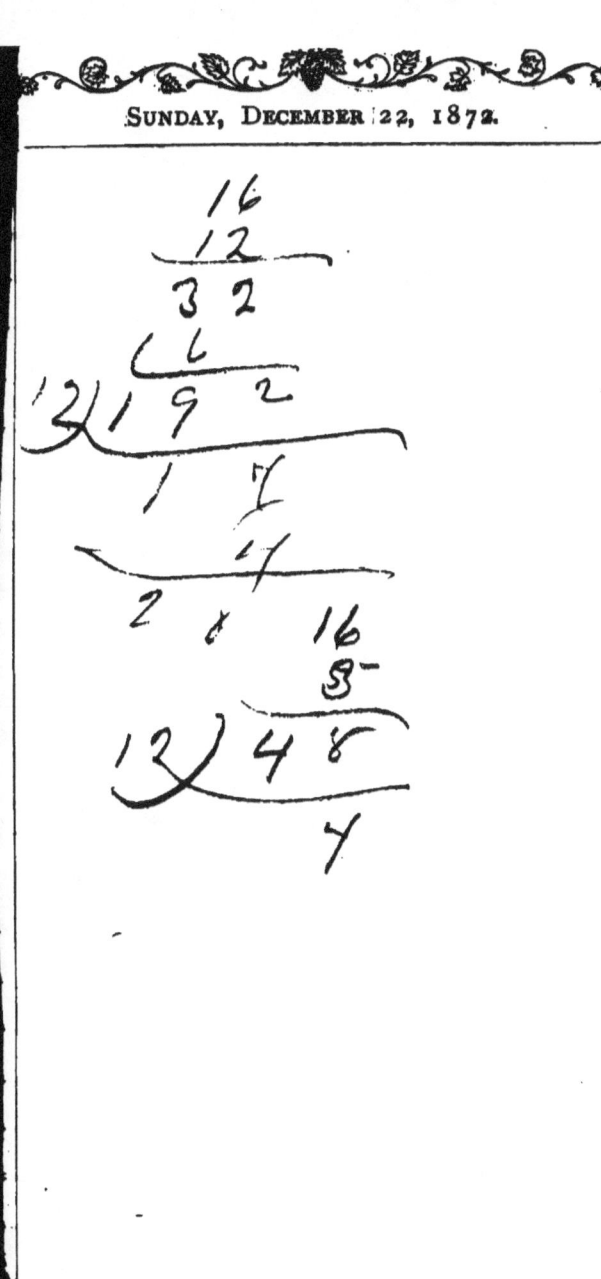

Tuesday, December 24, 1872.

WEDNESDAY, DECEMBER 25, 1872.

Saturday, December 28, 1872.

Sunday, December 29, 1872.

- 4 Cans Lard
- 1 Bushel B. Sugar
- Ginger
- Flour Ground
- Cinnamon
- Nutmeg
- Emerie Sermon
- Butter
- Salt Fish

Monday, December 30, 1872.

1.15
1.9

10.35

MEMORANDA.

Team Accounts
M. Carrick with 1 team,
Friday 29 March.
Duncan Campbell with
1 team Wednesday
April 3d.
J Martin with 1 team
Friday April 5.

MEMORANDA.

MEMORANDA.

1 Chinaman ½ day washing
work in orchard.

CASH ACCOUNT. JANUARY.

Date		Received	Paid
	From P. S. M	6 00	
April 12	" " " "	6 00	
" "	" " " "	5 00	
June	" "Father" "		
	" for Books	7 5 2	
" 14		10 00	
	" "		
	" G. H. Harris	20	
	" " " "	20 00	
Sep 11	" "	2	

$$\begin{array}{r}481\\105\text{-}\\\hline 2405\text{-}\\481\\\hline 505\ 505\text{-}\end{array}$$

CASH ACCOUNT. FEBRUARY.

Date.		Received.	Paid.
10	For a/c Book		1
14	For Educated		2
"	" Cigars		
"	" Postage-Stamps		

CASH ACCOUNT.   MARCH.

Date.		Received.	Paid

Received.	Paid.

I.

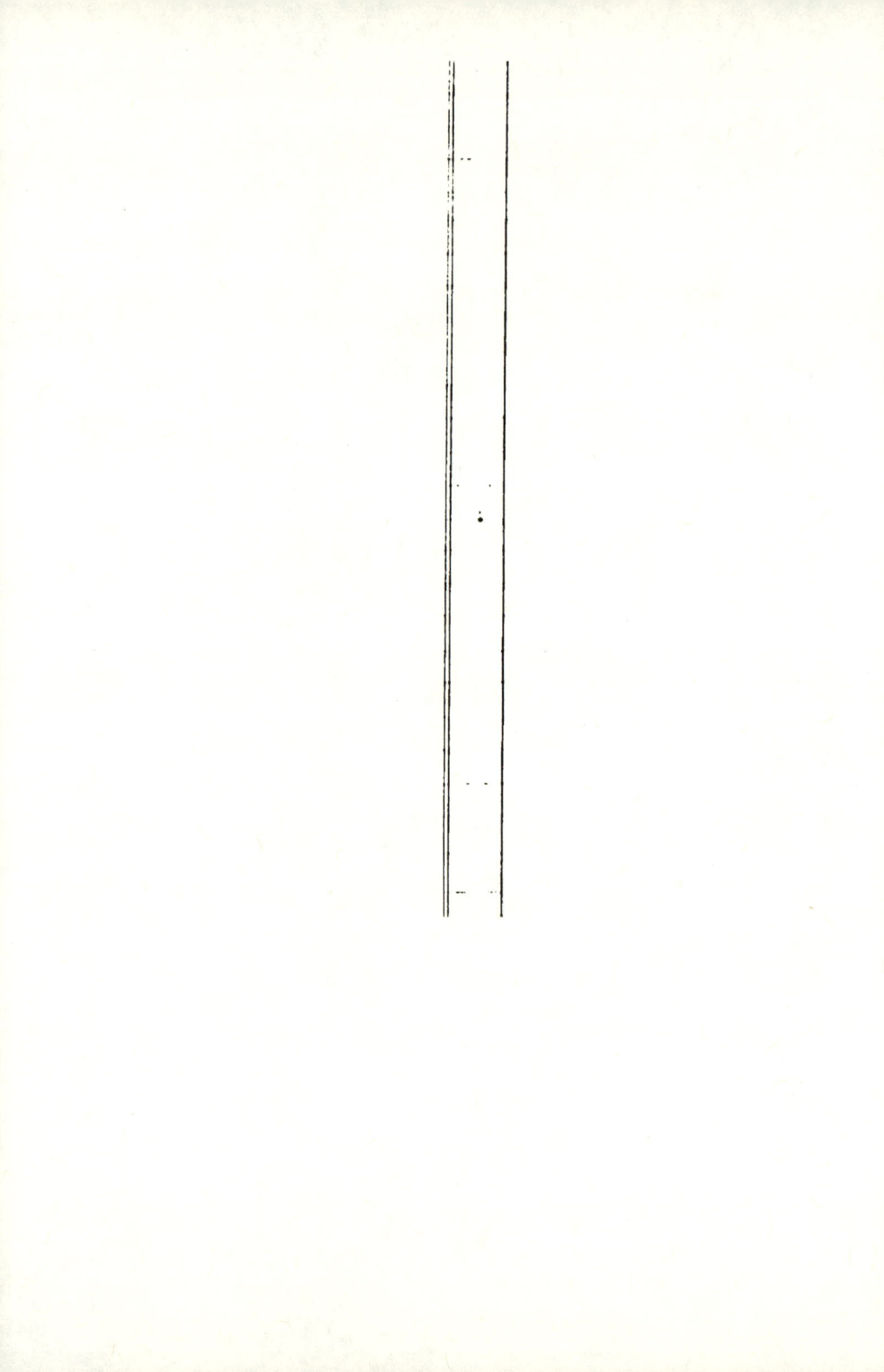

CASH ACCOUNT. MAY.

Date.	Received.	Paid.

CASH ACCOUNT. JUNE.

	Received.	Paid.

Date.		Received.	Paid.

ill [illegible]	
R.R. [illegible]	
China	1.00
[illegible]	.75
[illegible]	2.00
[illegible]	1.00
[illegible]	.35

	Received.	Paid.
B, R Henry 20 00		
" " " J 40 00		

Date.			Received.	Paid.

CASH ACCOUNT. SEPTEMBER.

Date		Received	Paid
	Pictures Places 3 in number, 2 ft 2 in ½ in length 21 in in width. And for same,		
	3 3		
	2 7		

CASH ACCOUNT.   OCTOBER.

Date.		Received.	Paid.

Received.	Paid.

CASH ACCOUNT. NOVEMBER.

Date.		Received.	Paid.

James Taylor.
Brohaskey Stab
San Jose.

CASH ACCOUNT. NOVEMBER.

Date.		Received.	Paid.
	S. P. Harvey	7 50	
	" " "	75 -	
	" " "	14 50	
	D. Campbell	20 -	
26	S. P. Harvey	1 50	

1 5 - 7 5

Feed Bros

5 = 5·18

5 - = 5 -

15 - 28

CASH ACCOUNT. DECEMBER.

Date.		Received.	Paid.

~~Maple sheet 24H 5 inches~~

Maple price
18 inches long
by 5 inches square

Maple for
rollers 5 in number
18 inches in length
and 1¾ diameter

$$
\begin{array}{r}
1.75 \\
\underline{325} \\
475 \\
65 \\
\underline{} \\
11575
\end{array}
$$

Fred Bro[?]

$ 5 = 818 $
$ 5 = 6.. $
$ 5 = 5.. $
$\overline{15\text{-}28}$

SUMMARY OF CASH ACCOUNT.

	Received.	Paid.
JAN.		
FEB.		
MAR.		
APR.		
MAY.		
JUNE.		
JULY.		
AUG.		
SEPT.		
OCT.		
NOV.		
DEC.		

MEMORANDA.

	Dollars.	Cts.

t Burley to
J M'Kewee to
the Ground
total figures

1 = 702
1 = 97
1 = 97
1 = 106
1 = 109
1 = 102
1 = 98
1 = 113
1 = 100
1 = 98
      1421
1 = 111
1 = 101
1 = 104
1 = 97
1 = 98
1 = 106
1 - 105

MEMORANDA.

Date.		Dollars.	Cts.
	Ant [illegible]		
	20 Sacks	20.55	—
	5 "	5.15	—
	5 "	5.16	—
		30.86	

There was
260 Sks in
ware house
when we
came here.

There was
4½ sks or
2 bbls Flour
when we
came here
part of a
Keg of
syrup.

MEMORANDA.

Date.		Dollars.	Cts.

12 Sk
Seed Barly
in ware
House
37 Sks Barly
[several?] [illegible]
29 Sk to
J McBevere
for to Seed

6-15 ~# Barly
to be Ground
30 5~# Burly
to be Ground
24 5~# Barly
to be Ground

106 ~#

MEMORANDA.

- A Life on the Ocean Wave
- Sleigh Shottische
- Newport
- Crystal Schottische
- Kate Kearney Waltz
- Job or Knob
- Pop goes the Weasel
- Charley over the water
- Rochester Schottische
- Irish wash woman
- White Cockade
- On the road to Boston

Date.		Dollars.	Cts.

    2 4 5
    9 7 2
    2 7 2
   _____
    6 7 7
    5 4 2 6
   _____
    ⌒ 2 8 3

MEMORANDA.

Date.		Dollars.

$$14.62$$
$$18.35$$
$$\overline{24.97}$$

$6\ 1/2$

$$2.25$$
$$6$$

$$2.25$$
$$6.50$$

$$2.25$$
$$6.5$$
$$1.125$$
$$135.0$$
$$\overline{14.625}$$

www.ingramcontent.com/pod-product-compliance
Lightning Source LLC
Chambersburg PA
CBHW030257240426
43673CB00040B/990